DAHLIA YVES

Money Magnet

Enter Your Abundant Era

Contents

1

Grim Reaper of Fear

When you lack money, it's constantly at the forefront of your mind, consuming all your energy as if money were the center of the universe. During times of financial strain, the brain enters a state of heightened alertness, similar to what our ancestors experienced, such as when cave dwellers were hypervigilant to be on guard for saber-toothed tigers. This preoccupation with financial security is a complex survival mechanism wired into our biological system of human survival instincts. This survival response floods our system with stress hormones, which limits our ability to think creatively or clearly so that we can reserve and use all of our mental energy to narrow our focus to immediate dangers such as the potential threat of a saber-toothed tiger. Our nervous system still responds to financial threats as if they are saber-toothed tigers in today's modern times. Our physiological human body translates this mental toll of financial insecurity as an oncoming saber-toothed tiger attacking and triggering us to a survival mode response. Fear is where we spiral into a cycle of panic & anxiety that becomes an all-consuming force that colors every decision and ripples through every aspect of our lives. Research in behavioral economics shows that financial stress can reduce our cognitive bandwidth by up to 13 IQ points—equivalent to losing a good night's sleep (Mani, 2013). Fear is how financial stress can take a toll on your energy levels even after getting your full 8 hours of necessitated sleep. Additional financial stress to your life is almost like you're behind on sleep even if you are technically clocking in your 8 hours of required sleep. This exemplifies how mental stress can hijack our brains, filling us with stress hormones that dumb down our decision-making abilities; even if we're trying to do the right thing by organizing our finances, it's like trying to do your financial planning after pulling an all-nighter. So, no wonder you're going through your days with a hazy mind and bad decisions like buying that sugary donut to relieve your stress because stress craves sugar!

But what if you can't even sleep because all your money worries are keeping you up at night & giving you panic attacks & nightmares? It's the middle of the night, and you feel a cocktail of emotions stirring within: feelings of anxiety, fear, unease, and uncertainty, waves of overwhelming emotions that feel dreadful to your soul. You're getting spooked by the Grim Reaper of Fear, where fears start to infiltrate every corner of your mind and possess you under a scarcity spell. The Grim Reaper of Fear is a villainous force of energy that preys on your fears and weaknesses, dragging you into a labyrinth of horrors of your imagination of worst-case scenarios, where every shadow becomes a potential threat that keeps you paranoid, living in a survival mode state of your daily life.

The Grim Reaper of Fear is the manifestation of your scarcity mindset. And all of your energy, even your creative energy, is feeding this scarcity mindset where instead of using your powers for the light, it is being leeched off by the Grim Reaper of Fear. The Grim Reaper of Fear lives off of fearful energy like a vampire; it sucks all your life force energy, leaving you feeling drained of your inner light. Its duty is to erode the courage and hope that sustains you, leaving you trapped in an inescapable web of terror. Like a loan shark, it preys on your moments of our deepest desperation, dragging you further into the abyss of bondage. It strips away your power and hope, leaving you trapped in a relentless cycle of fear and anxiety. This Grim Reaper of Fear casts a dark shadow over your entire life by keeping you in a state of lack & limitation.

But know this: the Grim Reaper of Fear only appears when you enter your scarcity mindset. Once you enter that realm of the scarcity mindset, you're stepping into a mental hell where the Grim Reaper of Fear lives at the seat of his throne. Remember, once you step foot in your scarcity mindset, you're stepping your foot into the home of the Grim Reaper of Fear, which is your mental hell, I tell ya! So even if it's a bad habit of yours, stop going there! Instead, shift your focus to an abundance mindset. This shift is not just a change in perspective, it's a transformation of your entire reality. It's a journey from fear to hope, from lack to plenty, and from survival to thriving. This shift is your key to unlocking a life of abundance and prosperity.

The Grim Reaper of Fear is a low vibe and so is your scarcity mindset. You see, you are like a radio, and when you're in scarcity mode, you're tuning into the worst radio station imaginable – 66.6 FEARS FM. This is a metaphor for the negative thoughts and fears that dominate your mind when you're in a scarcity mindset. It's your scarcity mindset that summons this Grim Reaper of Fear. The Grim Reaper of Fear and your scarcity mindset are on the same radio station, 66.6 FEARS FM. When you are in a scarcity mindset, you are tuning the voices in your head to the radio station of 66.6 FEARS FM, where the Grim Reaper of Fear is broadcasting all your fears and anxieties at full volume, drowning out any thoughts of possibility. The DJ is a dark demon, spinning hits like "You'll Never Be Enough," "Everything's About to Go Wrong," and "Who Do You Think You Are?" The Grim Reaper of Fear is the radio host of this station, showing up to block you from reaching your highest potential.

Everything we see and experience is an effect of a deeper cause. And what is that cause? Our minds. Our thoughts. It begins with a thought. Then, it turns into a belief that you take action, which leads to results that physically manifest into your physical reality. The whims of the universe don't dictate your current conditions; it's much more empowering. Behind every situation you face lies a silent cause. And that cause is you. Your mind. Your thoughts. Your actions and your energy. You are the creator of your reality. Every thought is like a seed, and that seed grows with more of the same repeated thoughts and energy you feed into it. It's suggested that humans have around 60,000 thoughts a day; how many of those thoughts are of fear, scarcity, & lack? Your thoughts are the beginning stages of manifestation. They are the seeds that plant your manifestations. Thoughts sprout the words you speak, actions you take, the energy you beam, and the reality you ultimately create.

We live in an energetic universe. Quantum physics, the study of the smallest particles of existence, reveals that everything is energy, vibrating at various frequencies. Our thoughts, emotions, and even our very essence as human beings are part of this grand vibrational universe. To understand our place in this energetic universe, we must delve into the frequencies that govern our existence, where love reigns at the highest frequency and fear at the lowest. So, when we are in a scarcity mindset, it means it's anchoring our energy down to the lowest vibrational frequency of *fear*. Basically, bad vibes vs. good vibes. Think about those mornings when your coffee spills, the barista gets your order wrong, and you're left grumbling all the way to work. If you stay fixated on that mistake and continue to stay upset, you're anchoring your energy in that low fear frequency, and guess what? The universe reflects like a mirror by responding with the same energy, leading to more mishaps in your day. Your spilled coffee spirals into a full-blown bad day because your energy just tuned to a station called "Bad

Vibes FM." Contrast that with the days when you're floating on cloud nine, maybe because you're in the honeymoon phase with a new lover. Everything feels happy, the world is more colorful, and the universe seems to conspire in your favor. That's because you're tuned into "High Vibes FM," broadcasting positivity and attracting more of the same high-vibe energy.

The Universe is like a giant mirror reflecting back the energy we project. This profound truth, woven into the fabric of reality, dictates that what we attract into our lives directly reflects our inner state. Quantum physics tells us that like frequencies attract like frequencies, and we are like radios, receiving the radio station to which channel we tune into with our energy. This is why when you enter a scarcity mindset, you anchor down to a low vibrational frequency and enter the portal of the Grim Reaper of Fear. It starts with negative thoughts that lead to bad feelings, and the next thing you know, you are in the energy of fear and low vibes.

A scarcity mindset keeps you in a perpetual loop of dreading what might go wrong. You're saying no to adventures, dreams, and love because you're terrified of losing, failing, & everything that could go wrong, etc. That's the reality of a scarcity mindset. It keeps you locked in a prison of your own making, convinced that the world is a dangerous, unfriendly place where you have to fight for every scrap. When you believe there's never enough, you operate from a place of lack. You make decisions based on fear rather than abundance. You say no to opportunities because you're afraid of failing. You hoard your time and energy because you're scared you won't have enough. You settle for crumbs because you don't believe you deserve the whole cake. This mindset tells you that there's a finite amount of everything in the world and that you must scramble and compete to get your share. It's a rotten lie that keeps you small and scared to live your life to the fullest.

Imagine you're holding a handful of sand. If you grip it too tightly, it slips through your fingers until there's nothing left. This is precisely what the scarcity mindset is: gripping, hoarding, controlling, and taking. You're so afraid of losing what you have that you squeeze it to death. This is the terrifying landscape of the scarcity mindset. It's a dark, dismal place where the air is thick with the fear of not having enough—enough time, enough money, enough love, enough success, enough happiness. You can't see past the thick smoke & smog of toxic beliefs. It's the alarming feeling that you're always one step away from disaster. It's why you clutch so tightly to what you have, afraid to let go and leap for more. Living with a scarcity mindset is like trying to drive with the emergency brake on. You can move barely forward, and it's a struggle. The constant fear of not having enough drags you down, slows your progress, and makes everything feel ten times harder than it needs to be. It's exhausting. The more you believe there's not enough, the more you attract situations that confirm that belief. You get stuck in a vicious cycle of lack and limitation.

But here's the truth! Did you know you had this manifestation power within you? That you are the creator of your reality. You might not have known it all this time, but you are manifesting all the time with your thoughts, actions, beliefs, and energy. Your thoughts and intentions are electrical impulses that are waves of energy rippling through the universe, creating and reshaping reality. It's like you're a human radio tower broadcasting your thoughts, feelings, and beliefs into the cosmos. And the universe is tuning in and responding to your signal. Remember, at the tiniest level, we're all just whirling clouds of energy connected to this grand web of this infinite universe of energy. You are not a passive participant in the game of life; you are the artist, the architect, the alchemist & the creator. And it's time you recognized the enormity of this power. The good news is you have free will to exercise your choices. You no longer have to be in place of the victim of the whims of circumstances; you can choose how you respond with your every thought, action, and energy.

Here's a reality check: you're giving away your power when you play the victim. You're saying, "Everything's happening to me," as if you are a mere pawn in this grand game of life. And that's a load of crap. The universe is not conspiring against you. It's simply responding to the energy you're radiating out into the field of space. If anything, the Universe conspires for you to learn and expand for the highest good for all! The Universe is an ally, a co-conspirator for your growth and expansion. If anything, the universe is conspiring for you to learn, evolve, and reach your highest self so that you can share and serve your special gifts that everyone can enjoy. Every challenge, setback, and heartbreak is an invitation to rise, harness your inner power, and transform lead into gold.

You are a powerful creator, capable of manifesting the most incredible, abundant life. The scarcity mindset and victim mentality are illusions, smoke, and mirrors designed to keep you playing small and block you from your truth. Remember, manifestation isn't always instant. It's like planting a seed: you don't see the sprout immediately, but beneath the soil, magic is happening. Be patient and nurture your dreams with positive thoughts, words, actions, and energy.

2

Subconscious Mind

The subconscious mind, often called the powerhouse of our thoughts and beliefs, plays a crucial role in writing our money stories, which affects attracting financial abundance. It's responsible for shaping our beliefs, attitudes, and behaviors around money, ultimately influencing our ability to create wealth in adulthood. The subconscious mind is like a library archive of personal memories that have developed our thoughts, beliefs, and intricate life patterns through adulthood, shaping the reasons behind our actions and decisions. Scientists have discovered that our conscious mind, which is responsible for only about 5% of our thoughts and actions, pales in comparison to the power of the subconscious mind, which is responsible for 95% of the workings of our mind. The subconscious mind shapes our beliefs, habits, and, ultimately, our financial reality until we develop our consciousness regarding wealth. Understanding and mastering this process is crucial for achieving financial success. Manifesting money using your subconscious mind involves reprogramming your mind for a steadfast relationship with wealth consciousness.

Have you ever noticed the uncanny way money seems to gravitate toward some folks while others perpetually scrape the bottom of the barrel? That's no cosmic accident, my friend. It's a glaring insight into the way the subconscious mind works. Those "lucky" folks who attract wealth believe, at a deep, fundamental level, that they deserve it. They've got a solid relationship with money, treating it like a welcome guest, not a meddling intruder in the subconscious mind department. They've got a peachy money brain groove path for money to stroll in on a red carpet for a welcoming party to their personal bank account. This means they have neural pathways in the brain that carry chemical neural messages that say, "I love money," "I am rich, "I can have it," "I deserve good things," & "I am worthy," etc. Now, compare these neural pathways to your most commonly held money beliefs. How often do you say, "I'm broke," "I can't afford this," "I don't deserve that," "That's too expensive," etc.? These messages subconsciously block you from receiving money. The brain's neural pathways for those messages become stronger through repetition. Those corresponding neural pathways are reinforced when we repeatedly engage in specific thoughts, behaviors, and emotions. The more you think, say, & believe these mantras, the more they manifest in your reality.

Your not-so-glamorous financial situation isn't solely just from living paycheck to paycheck or your nine-to-five drudgery. It's way deeper in the roots of your subconscious mind that controls your personal finance drama show like a puppeteer. Your subconscious mind runs the show behind the curtains, directing your personal "Money Melodrama" like a seasoned Broadway director. Your subconscious mind directs your financial narrative until you decide to update the program from the year you were born to the year you are in now.

Neural pathways are thought patterns that become deeply ingrained in our minds and program our subconscious mind - which influences our actions often without our conscious awareness. Neural pathways that are repeatedly activated reinforce the default ways in which we think, feel, and act. Therefore, whatever words you say the most about money create the strongest neural pathways that build your subconscious programming. These pathways become the lenses you are prescribed when navigating your life regarding money. They develop your core beliefs, habits, & behaviors that confirm your subconscious beliefs. Subconscious patterns, once set, can create a loop of self-reinforcement. For instance, a person with ingrained low self-esteem might consistently view situations reflecting this belief. Their perspective, rooted in their subconscious, navigates life through a lens crafted by these deeply embedded subconscious beliefs and collects more evidence, further solidifying their low self-esteem.

Much of our subconscious programming is rooted in the experiences from our early years of childhood. During this formative period, our brains are exceptionally receptive, absorbing the beliefs and behaviors imparted by our caregivers, environment, and culture around us. These influences become deeply embedded in our subconscious mind, shaping our perspectives and actions well into adulthood. It's a startling realization: the notions instilled in us as children may still steer our lives as adults. This is particularly true regarding our self-worth and our financial habits. The subconscious mind is less about our conscious desires and more about our ingrained subconscious beliefs. It's a reservoir of the narratives we absorbed in childhood, narratives that have since congealed into a foundation of beliefs that underlie our current reality. Thus, our relationship with money, along with many other aspects of our lives, often reflects these deep-seated subconscious beliefs.

Our brains, constantly besieged by a deluge of sensory inputs, employ an unconscious filtering mechanism to manage this onslaught. This filtration is more than a mere neurological process; it shapes our sub-conscious programming by determining which pieces of information we deem important and decide to retain. Within this selective process, emotionally charged information stands out. Events, experiences, or data that evoke strong emotions, whether joyous or distressing, tend to etch themselves more deeply in our memories. Emotions act as markers, signaling the brain that the information is of personal significance and essential to our survival. Hence, our subconscious is not just a passive recipient but a selective curator, focusing on what resonates with our emotional core. Emotions serve as a signal to the brain that the information has personal relevance.

Imagine your subconscious as a sponge, absorbing experiences since your earliest days. It gleans meaning from everything - interactions with parents, the marketing of television commercials, and especially traumatic events like when your pet hamster, Mr. Peanut, went missing, leading you to rue your financial constraints such as a lack of financial resources to buy a better cage. What's crucial to understand is that events laden with intense emotions carve deeper grooves in our neural pathways. Traumatic or emotionally charged experiences forge stronger neuronal connections, embedding specific beliefs into our subconscious. Consequently, painful memories, especially those linked to financial matters, can instill a deep-seated belief that money is inherently troublesome or negative. This process illustrates how our earliest and most emotional experiences shape our subconscious attitudes toward money and other significant aspects of life.

Picture your subconscious mind as a deeply intuitive, ever-reliable emotional compass driven by an expansive archive of your life's experiences. Imagine it as a vast, intricately organized library—every chapter of your story is stored there, from triumphs and heartbreaks to fleeting moments of joy, like when you laughed at a silly cat video decades ago. Each experience is carefully cataloged, ready to subtly influence your choices and guide your future decisions, no matter how monumental or trivial.

Your conscious mind simply doesn't have the bandwidth to handle this overwhelming volume of information while managing your daily life. That's where your subconscious steps in, acting as the quiet archivist working behind the scenes. It ensures that every piece of data, every emotion, and every lesson learned is stored away for the moments you need it most—whether in a crisis or the seemingly unrelated but profoundly connected situations life throws your way.

When trauma strikes and becomes too overwhelming for your conscious mind to process, your subconscious steps in to protect you. It locks those painful memories away in a metaphorical safe, safeguarding them until the time is right—until your mind and body feel secure enough to handle them. This mechanism isn't always comfortable but is essential for emotional survival and growth.

This system allows your subconscious to connect dots you might never consciously see. For example, the grief of losing your childhood hamster, Mr. Peanut, and the realization that an exorbitant cage might have saved him could later prepare you to manage the complexities of saving for something far more profound—like funding your parent's funeral planning. It's something you might never have planned for until death enters your life and makes you think of the unthinkable. These seemingly unrelated events reflect the intricate wisdom of your subconscious mind, weaving together life's lessons in ways that may only make sense in hindsight. It works tirelessly to keep you grounded, resilient, and prepared for life's unexpected turns.

This brilliant orchestration of your subconscious mind transforms seemingly simple experiences into profound life lessons, storing them like time capsules that open precisely when needed. Every heartbreak, every triumph, every seemingly insignificant moment becomes part of a vast wisdom network, ready to illuminate your path through life's most challenging territories.

Your subconscious isn't just a passive storage system—it's an active meaning-maker, constantly weaving new connections between past and present, loss and learning, small moments, and life's most significant decisions. It works silently but ceaselessly, ensuring that no experience, however painful or seemingly trivial, goes to waste for the story of your life.

In the vast landscape of your life experiences, your inner alarm system operates at lightning speed, pulling up files from the archives of your personal history to make sense of your current scenarios of life events. However, your subconscious doesn't consistently deliver a precise translation that can be applied to your current circumstances. For example, back to the scene of the death of Mr. Peanut when you were just 7 years old, totally innocent and unaware, facing the heart-wrenching loss of your furry best friend. In that intense moment, your subconscious, like a forensic photographer, snaps a quick pic and slaps a label on it: 'The Day My Heart Broke Over Mr. Peanut.'

Now, plot twist - our kiddo was sipping on a soda at that exact tear-jerking moment. The subconscious, being its quirky connector, makes a note. Fast forward, and voilà – even as an adult, every time they see that brand of soda, their heart twists and turns. Why? That's how triggers are born. Because their inner subconscious brain has filed that soda under 'Emotional Heartbreak – Pet Edition.' The subconscious noted where, from that day forward, that little kiddo may forever associate soda with the anguish of loss. Fast forward to adulthood, and the sight of that same soda can trigger an involuntary shudder, a reminder of that "death of a beloved pet" file tucked away in the depths of their subconscious. This illustrates how seemingly unrelated elements can become entwined in our subconscious, influencing our reactions in unforeseen ways. Understanding this subconscious programming can explain how our lives in ways can seem arbitrary but are deeply rooted in our emotional history if we dare to take a deep analysis. The subconscious mind is a supercomputer that takes information to repurpose it for our future well-being. On the other hand, it can also manifest emotional triggers that might not feel logical or immediately clear.

Let's focus on a topic that often eludes clear understanding: money and the subconscious. Consider how negative emotions about wealth might be hidden deep within your psyche like an innocuous soda symbolizes loss. Tucked away in the nooks and crannies of your mind might be a whole saga of money-related emotional roller coasters or chaotic financial fireworks. If money is associated with past traumas or negative experiences, it can become a source of chaos or anxiety versus a source of positivity or security. Delving into these subconscious associations is essential to reshape your financial perspective.

Your childhood experiences with money may have been unconsciously processed as negative rather than positive. Buried in your subconscious could be numerous instances where money was linked to emotional pain or chaos. Childhood interactions with money might have been internalized as a series of disheartening emotions, failing to cultivate a constructive attitude toward finances. Within the depths of your subconscious might lie memories of familial financial disputes, the emotional distress tied to money matters, or the disorders that seemed to accompany financial issues. Your younger self might have seen money as a drama queen, thanks to all those family squabbles over bills or the emotional tornadoes that swirled around payday. These moments are like tracks on the subconscious playlist, setting the rhythm for how you interact with money today. Our lives are shaped mainly by the programming of our subconscious minds formed from our childhood. These experiences create a complex tapestry in our subconscious, influencing our attitudes and behaviors toward money today.

If you grapple with financial challenges, you've likely unwittingly hoisted clandestine money baggage. Think back to your formative years – did you incessantly encounter refrains like "money doesn't grow on trees" or "we're not made of money"? Perhaps you were regaled with tales of the wealthy, painted as innately selfish or morally askew, forging a subconscious link between affluence and malevolence. Your subconscious mind, ever the efficient filter, distilled these impressions into a single equation: money equals bad. And naturally, you've been hardwired to evade the bad. After all, bad equals pain, and our primal human instincts urge us to steer clear of pain at all costs. This belief system is more than just a psychological construct; it's a survival mechanism. We're programmed to avoid pain; if money is perceived as "bad," it becomes something to evade. This subconscious narrative, written mainly during your formative years, has the power to shape your adult financial experiences. Your subconscious may have crystallized these notions into a detrimental belief: that money is inherently bad. Without realizing it, you may have set the stage for a narrative rife with economic hardships stemming from a deep-seated, yet hidden, conviction about the nature of wealth and money. Thus, your adult life is scripted as a dolorous tale of financial miseries, all thanks to this covert subconscious narrative you've unwittingly authored about money.

One common myth that once held me captive was the infamous "starving artist's saga." My subconscious convinced me that money and creativity were like oil and water – fundamentally incompatible. So, as my subconscious programming followed suit, I followed this narrative until one miraculous day, I had an epiphany: it was all just a myth, a story – a fictional screenplay crafted for those who, whether consciously or unconsciously, chose to buy into it and then allowed it to play this movie as my life. Whatever story you narrate in your mind is the story, the script you play the main character in life, and it manifests in your reality. It's high time we liberate ourselves from these antiquated scripts and remnants of generational fears about money and cease allowing them to dictate the course of our prospective futures that are genuinely brimming with boundless opportunities! It's time to hit that "unsubscribe" button on those scary stories we have been telling ourselves for years of scarcity, fear, and lack of money.

How many of us are clearly aware of our own hidden beliefs, deep down, that money is evil? Or is it something that 'other' people have? How many of us have been told that 'money doesn't grow on trees' and started seeing it as a scarce & limited resource? How many of us feel separate from money?

We form these beliefs without knowing it, letting our subconscious mind take the wheel as it drives to the money desert while we sit in the backseat blindfolded, wondering why we haven't reached the ocean of financial haven. But before you blame it all on your under-the-hood wiring, let's give the subconscious mind some spotlight for its superpowers. The purpose of the subconscious mind is to regulate bodily functions automatically. It's in charge of the things we take for granted—like our little heartbeats drumming away, the seamless expansion and contraction of our lungs, our digestive system, well, digesting – and it does it all without us needing to think about it consciously. It's our unseen, behind-the-scenes ally, tirelessly working while you're plotting world domination (or, you know, figuring out your budget). It's like the universe's gift, all without you having to give it a second thought. Imagine if you had to micromanage all that. If we had to control all these bodily functions consciously, we'd be too swamped to imagine getting through an episode of our favorite Netflix series. That's why our subconscious mind takes care of our autonomic systems, and our conscious mind takes care of more cerebral thinking tasks that require more conscious efforts. The subconscious is conducting these autonomic systems, freeing your conscious mind to take on more novel tasks, like daydreaming and being more creative. Your subconscious is like a backstage crew at a concert - setting the stage for your conscious mind to jam out with creativity and intuition and, yes, plan those big, juicy financial goals.

Keep in mind that your subconscious mind is awake and active all the time. It's your nocturnal watchman; it takes care of everything, so you don't have to relearn something every time you acquire a new skill. You know how it is when you're learning something new, and everything feels confusing and uncomfortable? But after countless hours of practice and swearing, you're suddenly a pro, and then one day, you can suddenly do your new skill even with your eyes closed. With relentless practice, what once seemed insurmountable becomes effortless, almost instinctual. That is your subconscious mind's power. When you repeatedly practice something, like driving, it learns it into memory and becomes second nature. It resembles automation in the workplace in that once a machine is programmed, it operates automatically.

The subconscious is a tireless sentinel, diligently cataloging experiences and overseeing your body's myriad functions. The subconscious mind is your very own data bank, working 24/7. Consider the subconscious mind a tape recorder and an ever-active, internal repository. It chronicles every detail, with emotionally charged events leaving the deepest imprints. Traumas, seared into memory by their particularly potent emotional intensity, are locked away in some hidden corner of your mind. The subconscious uses these memories as lessons, guiding you away from repeating any past mishaps. Thus arise triggers and flashbacks, relics of our mind's survival instinct. They are part of an ancient protective mechanism, alerting us to hazards we once faced. It's like having an internal alarm system that buzzes whenever you encounter something that once spelled danger. This explains common fears like heights, spiders, and rats – ancestral fears etched into our being to shield us from harm. These fears, woven into our genetic fabric, can trigger a visceral reaction to flying on a plane or seeing a spider. From evolution, ancestral DNA has been encoded into our biology to protect us today using fear to avoid what our ancestors died for, like the black plague and falling off cliffs. These triggering protective fear responses still guard us today, turning our forebears' life-or-death experiences into life-saving instincts. Your subconscious, whether unconscious aversion to signs of illness or an instinctive caution, is ever watchful, striving to avert danger and preserve your well-being.

The subconscious loves the *path of least resistance*, so it tends to follow the same patterns. For example, you've likely developed a distinct approach to routine tasks, like brushing your teeth or navigating your daily commute, or even those wonderfully quirky habits that make you, well, you. This also goes for the thoughts in your head. Humans have around 60,000 thoughts a day, most of which are the same thoughts from the day before. So, remember your favorite song lyrics, your grandma's delicious secret pancake recipe, and that cringe moment from 7th grade? It's just the same with your money stories. Just like that tune, you know, the one that keeps playing in your head? You're replaying thought tunes that say, "Rich people are snobs" or "I'm broke but noble."

Don't merely settle for that initial money story your subconscious penned from when your parents were arguing over money when you were simply 5 years old. It's time to embark on a profound transformation, crafting a blockbuster movie that reverberates with the triumphant notes of wellness and financial joy. Author this new narrative from the perspective of the new, evolved and wiser you to manifest your life's plot line and take a thrilling turn towards abundance and harmony!

To forge lasting change, you must summon the courage to expand your comfort zone, akin to the moment you embark on something entirely new – like stepping into a new career. There's always that initial hurdle of awkwardness, discomfort, and the uncharted territory of the unknown. Likewise, anticipate a learning curve when it comes to transforming your financial landscape. You must venture beyond your comfort's cozy confines to usher in more income – whether by negotiating a raise, seizing a promotion, or embracing additional responsibilities. To enact profound shifts in your life, you must grow by bursting out of that comfort bubble! Assume the role of the CEO of your mind and take charge of your subconscious by curbing its inclination to gravitate towards the safe comfort zones of the familiar. Persist until your newfound beliefs about abundance become the cornerstone of your new beliefs. Make a conscious choice to evict those pesky bad habits obstructing your path to wealth and throw a grand housewarming celebration for abundant habits you're diligently constructing in your mental realm!

And finally, commit to this new narrative. Your subconscious has been grooving to the old tune for a long time, so don't be surprised if it tries to snap back to the familiar old station. Remember, it loves the path of least resistance -whatever is familiar and comfortable. The subconscious mind feels the most safe in what it knows versus the unfamiliar. Even if it seems perplexing why you might slip back into those old, detrimental habits, your subconscious interprets it as a return to comfort. It may not make logical sense, but to your subconscious, "overspending" could feel more comfortable because that's what it's accustomed to doing when stress enters your life. Your subconscious mind operates by one of the languages known as habits, those routine behaviors that fill so much of your day. Remember, the subconscious mind operates automatically because it handles numerous autonomic processes without requiring conscious awareness or deliberate effort. Your habits are primarily automatic, whether you consistently grab your toothbrush first thing in the morning or complain about your day.

Now, how does this awe-inspiring subconscious mind work to help us? Just like any good personal assistant, it does its best work when given clear instructions. You need to communicate with it in a language it understands – and that language is emotion and repetition. Emotion is the power switch that turns your thoughts and ideas into subconscious commands, and repetition is the training program that ensures those commands stick.

Your subconscious mind is also a pro at problem-solving, working in the background while you're out there conquering the world, coming up with solutions like a nutty professor. Have you ever had a brilliant idea? Do ideas come to you while you're taking a shower or right before you go to sleep? Your subconscious is taking on solutions creatively at that moment! Your subconscious mind is a strong ally that is always willing to help. Your reality will be created depending on the beliefs and thoughts you feed it. You may train your subconscious to help you create a life that inspires you to leap out of bed in the morning and chase your wildest dreams with deliberate intention. Your subconscious mind can be your partner in crime for manifesting the life of your dreams. It can take all your beliefs, thoughts, feelings, and input and create a reality that mirrors those inputs. If you're always thinking, "I'm a financial disaster," guess what? Your subconscious mind will help you maintain your role as a financial disaster of the year. But if you switch that to "I'm a money magnet," the universe better watch out because here you come!

There is a powerful force that lies in the deep, subjective thoughts that shape your life: the subconscious mind. Your future is scripted by the deep, powerful thoughts rooted in your subconscious mind. It's the core, heartfelt thoughts that mold your reality. It's not enough to think, "I am great." You've got to think great thoughts consistently and deeply, affecting your subconscious mind and core beliefs. Just spouting affirmations about being healthy or brilliant won't cut it. Your subconscious has to buy in, which takes more than surface-level self-talk. To truly change, you must dive beyond your surface opinions and reprogram your subconscious mind.

The key to harnessing the power of the subconscious mind lies in consistent practice and repetition. Gradually integrating subconscious techniques into our daily routine allows us to rewire our minds for financial success. It is important to remember that manifesting money is not solely about wishful thinking; it requires taking inspired action and seizing opportunities that arise.

Say you want to overcome your phobia of speaking in front of groups of people. Your subconscious mind will eventually update its records if you expose yourself to public speaking regularly and link pleasant feelings with the experience (such as the pleasure of engaging the audience, the joy of sharing your ideas, or even the satisfaction of making it through another speech). It will begin to support your new conviction that public speaking is a meaningful and enjoyable activity rather than a deathly nightmare. Remember, you have undone and untangled a cord of beliefs since birth, so you might not even know what beliefs you are dealing with and what truths will be revealed along your healing journey.

So start with investigating your past first. Identify your stories about money acquired from your family, friends, and environment as a child. Confront them and rewrite them. Replace these narratives with ones that serve you and make you feel alive, excited, and inspired. Whenever you think, "I can't afford that," switch to "How can I afford that?" This shift forces your brain to get creative and look for solutions instead of dwelling on problems. Create affirmations, mantras, rituals, or anything that gives you a buzz and makes you feel inspired about money.

It's time to take charge, sit in the director's chair, and construct the financial reality you want. So, work with your subconscious mind by fully understanding how it is wired and giving precise instructions to code it for abundance and for your greatest desires to manifest.

Practice mindfulness, get restful sleep, and create a ritual and space for relaxation and free thinking to tap into the potential of your subconscious mind. In these moments of restful breaks, answers will smack you upside the head outta nowhere. Sparks will light up when you're chilling in the shower or spacing out on your morning run. The subconscious mind holds your secret treasure trove of personal memories you don't consciously remember, but that doesn't mean it's not there, quietly influencing your problem-solving and creative abilities from the shadows. It's your hidden superpower, the silent genius that plays with the blocks of your experiences, knowledge, and emotions and invents something mind-bogglingly transformative. It's making castles out of grains of thought you didn't even know you had. It's communicating via intuition, pointing you in the right direction even when you feel clueless—ever had a hunch, a gut feeling? Yeah, that's your subconscious behind the scenes, waving flags and firing flares, guiding you through your intuitive feelings. Remember, your subconscious mind is also your super-smart co-pilot, navigating the twists and turns of this roller coaster ride of a life.

3

Total Money-Mindset Makeover

You can use the power of your subconscious mind to work for you and in your favor by reprogramming it to believe you are superhuman to reach your highest potential. Imagine your subconscious as a supercomputer, programming shaped by childhood experiences, societal influences, and cultural myths. Stealthy and powerfully influential, these invisible scripts have been orchestrating your financial reality for years, shaping your beliefs about money, wealth, and even your worth.

But here's the thrilling twist: you're not just a passenger in this story—you're the programmer. Those childhood moments, like watching your parents stretch every penny or absorbing myths such as "money is the root of all evil," weren't fleeting. They carved neural pathways into your brain, forming a mental map that still governs your financial reality. Yet, within this realization lies immense power: you can rewrite the code. You can code the supercomputer of your subconscious mind to reach your highest potential.

When you work on your money mindset, you're diving into the intricate process of reverse-engineering your subconscious to decode the hidden mechanics of your money psyche. This isn't about dollars and cents—it's about uncovering the emotional and mental relics of your "money mindset" and boldly rewriting your financial narrative. Think of it as a full-on mental remodel. Visualizations of abundance, affirmations of worth, and gratitude practices aren't just feel-good exercises—they're tools of neuroscience, rewiring your brain, firing up new synaptic connections, and carving fresh pathways that create new beliefs such as *Yes, I am worthy of wealth!* to manifest new realities.

But let's keep it real: you don't leap from scarcity to swimming in gold coins overnight. Building wealth is more like training for a marathon than chasing a quick sprint. You stretch your "wealth comfort zone" incrementally, embracing small wins—a $1,000 milestone today, $10,000 tomorrow—allowing your nervous system to adapt without tripping the wires of self-sabotage.

The fascinating truth about sudden wealth—like winning the lottery—is that it can send your nervous system into overdrive. Studies reveal that most lottery winners lose fortunes within a few short years. Why? Because beneath the glittering jackpot lies the hidden challenges that come with it, and many people aren't prepared to handle money that wasn't earned with intention and connection to meaning.

Imagine this: one moment, you've never seen more than a few thousand dollars in your account, and the next—BOOM—there's a million bucks staring back at you. Your nervous system hits overdrive, your brain short-circuits, and suddenly, it's chaos. You're buying your cousin a Lamborghini, treating yourself to a yacht, and booking that dream home in Bora Bora. But then come the unexpected bills, bad investments, and a whirlwind of impulsive decisions that drain your fortune before you even realize it. Why? Because you weren't *ready*. You didn't have the emotional or mental framework to receive and hold in a safe space for that sudden abundance. If you aren't ready—if you don't feel safe, confident, and aligned with a clear plan for managing and directing that money—it will start to slip through your fingers, flowing out of your life as quickly as it arrived.

This isn't just bad luck; it's the energetic nature of money at play. Money, like everything else in the Universe, is energy. It gravitates toward those who understand it and are prepared to nurture it. You may have successfully manifested the jackpot, but without aligning with the energy of stewardship and purpose, you haven't manifested the ability to *keep* it.

Let's get real: do you genuinely want to win the lottery, or is it just a shortcut putting a band-aid to cover a deeper wound? Spoiler alert—your soul didn't sign up for this earthly experience just to chase Powerball dreams. You came here with a unique, incredible purpose beyond financial windfalls. When you align with that purpose, the Universe responds accordingly and begins delivering the resources, including money, you need in the right amounts and at the right time. When you align with your true purpose, everything else—resources, opportunities, even financial abundance—will naturally flow to you.

Mistakes with money, whether it's racking up debt on $10,000 or overspending a minor windfall, aren't failures—they're lessons. The Universe uses these moments to teach and prepare you for greater abundance. Every financial stumble—whether it's blowing through $10,000, racking up credit card debt, or living paycheck to paycheck— isn't a failure. It's training. The Universe is preparing you to handle the $100,000, $1,000,000, or more coming your way. These moments are cosmic interventions, asking, *"Are you ready to be a wise steward of your blessings yet?"* Each financial misstep carries wisdom, shaping your ability to handle the $100,000, $1 million, or more destined for you when you're ready to receive it with clarity and purpose.

Instead of chasing lottery fantasies, focus on building the foundation that aligns with your higher purpose. The key isn't just wealth but alignment. When you honor your unique purpose, the Universe will conspire to support you—not just with money, but with everything you need to fulfill your highest calling. Dream big, take intentional actions, and pay attention to the lessons money teaches you. When you're truly ready—not just in your wallet but in your spirit—the Universe will open the floodgates. And this time, you'll be prepared to catch every drop and dance joyfully in the downpour, knowing you're aligned with the life you're meant to live. So, instead of chasing quick riches, chase authenticity and alignment. That's when the magic truly happens, and the wealth you manifest will not only come but flow like a river.

Let's get one thing straight: manifesting wealth isn't about sitting around, crossing your fingers, and hoping a bag of money falls into your lap. It's about leveling up your wealth game by mastering your mindset. It's an active pursuit that develops your wealth consciousness. It's about forging a powerful partnership between your conscious and subconscious minds, a synergy guided by the wisdom of meditation, the overflowing gratitude in your heart, and the conscientiousness of mindfulness. By silencing the relentless chatter of your monkey mind and turning up the volume on positive thinking, you send out a wave of high energy to attract abundance —positive vibrations that attract the riches of the universe into your reality.

This is an empowering process of crafting a money mindset overhaul. It's the art of adopting a mindset that radiates abundance, gratitude, and limitless possibilities. You become the fearless warrior of your own transformation through unwavering dedication to practicing these subconscious techniques. In this thrilling rewiring of the mind, the neurons in your brain rewrite their score, creating new, harmonious melodies of thoughts that resonate with the magnetic energy of abundance.

Believe it with every fiber of your being because manifesting money through the immense power of your subconscious can radically transform your life. Imagine your subconscious as a magnetic force, tirelessly drawing and shaping the experiences and circumstances that align with the vibration of your dominant thoughts and beliefs.

If you've been clutching onto limiting beliefs like "money is scarce" or "I don't deserve financial abundance," it's time for a revolution. Through intricate rituals of affirmations, vivid mental imagery, and consistent subconscious exercises, you're reshaping the very essence of your thoughts and beliefs about money. By continually feeding your subconscious with empowering and radiant thoughts, you effortlessly sync your vibration with the frequency of abundance, making the attraction of financial prosperity a positive experience led by the fearless spirit of your transformational mind.

Diving into subconscious manifestation techniques opens an electrifying avenue toward attracting abundance. Venture deep into the subconscious with practices like meditation, visualization, and powerful energy work to transform your mind's power. These practices connect us to the grand universal flow of abundance, aligning our very essence with its abundant frequency. And what happens when we align with this energy? We become magnetic, drawing in financial opportunities and life-changing experiences that elevate our prosperity to new heights.

Picture this transformation as crafting a masterpiece, stroke by stroke. Each affirmation, visualization, and moment of gratitude builds a vibrant picture of abundance that realigns your actions to the limitless opportunities you are attuned to. Suddenly, doors of opportunities swing wide open, and life's challenges become stepping stones instead of stumbling blocks.

The magic truly ignites when you can hold this abundant mindset through the ups and downs of life. Whether the financial tide rises or falls, you become the skilled surfer who navigates with grace, balance, and unshakable belief. This isn't about chasing fleeting highs or wishful thinking—it's about stepping into the architect role, reprogramming your reality, and creating a life of sustainable financial mastery you own with confidence, joy, and purpose.

Now, let's embark on this thrilling money mindset makeover journey. First, we must observe the connection between our thoughts and emotions and the results we witness in our financial lives. By spotlighting our thoughts and beliefs about money, we uncover sneaky patterns that may have stealthily sabotaged our economic success. But here's the good news – with unwavering commitment and a dash of discipline, we can embark on the adventure of reprogramming our subconscious. We're tossing aside those old limitations, like snakes shedding their old skin, and flinging ourselves wide open to the unlimited, tantalizing possibilities of financial abundance available for all.

Total Money-Mindset Makeover Strategies

Hypnosis

To elevate your self-worth and transform your identity directly in your subconscious mind, begin with self-hypnosis. Through the miraculous world of hypnosis to reprogram the subconscious mind, we're setting ourselves free to welcome the grand river of prosperity into our lives. This isn't some magical hocus-pocus, but a pathway to harness the immense power of your subconscious, a path that could reshape your financial reality.

Imagine yourself in a serene state of profound relaxation, like you've unlocked the secret chamber of your mind—a vault filled with the potential to rewrite the story of your financial life. In this tranquil mental space, you plant the seeds of new beliefs and thought patterns that seamlessly align with your financial dreams. Through guided hypnosis sessions, you shatter the chains of limiting beliefs, dismantle the barriers to financial riches, and harmonize your subconscious thoughts to align with beliefs of prosperity to manifest. It's a symphonic transformation where you replace the old, constrictive beliefs with new, empowering ones, carving out a clear path toward financial abundance in your mind. It's almost like you're recording a new movie over an unused VHS tape.

The real magic unfolds when you understand the dynamic linkage between your subconscious mind and the manifestation of your financial beliefs. With its specific techniques, hypnosis grants you access to your deep subconscious by bypassing the conscious gatekeeper, allowing direct communication with your subconscious. Here, you sow the seeds of abundant beliefs and cut the weeds of scarcity and limiting beliefs, ensuring your desires take root deep within your psyche and effortlessly sprout into your reality.

Let's demystify hypnosis. It's not about mystical incantations or mind control—it's a powerhouse tool that gives you access to the profound depths of your subconscious. In the context of financial prosperity, it's all about understanding how hypnosis works and its profound influence on rewiring your subconscious mind and limiting beliefs. At its core, hypnosis is a state of deep relaxation and heightened focus—a doorway to your subconscious mind. Contrary to common myths, it's not about relinquishing control; it's about heightened receptivity, where your conscious mind takes a step back and opens a secret passageway, allowing your subconscious to welcome suggestions and ideas with receptivity.

Think of your subconscious mind as a sponge, soaking up every experience and information you've encountered throughout your life, including your beliefs about money and financial success. Unfortunately, these beliefs are often deeply ingrained and limiting, chaining you to a cycle of scarcity. But the beauty of hypnosis lies in bypassing the vigilant conscious mind to work directly with the subconscious. It's like pruning all the weeds of limiting beliefs, uncovering and releasing any negative patterns or beliefs that have held you back from financial prosperity. Then, additional techniques such as guided visualizations, affirmations, and positive suggestions serve as tools to rewrite your money stories, forging new neural pathways that resonate with abundance and wealth. By consistently reinforcing these positive suggestions, you create lasting change in your subconscious, inviting financial abundance to flow effortlessly into your life.

Remember that hypnosis is a state of deep relaxation and heightened focus—a gateway to your subconscious, where the true magic of transformation unfolds. Crafting your personalized hypnosis script is paramount. Find a serene, distraction-free space, close your eyes, breathe deeply, and allow your body to relax. As you slip into this tranquil state, focus on your financial aspirations. Visualize yourself already living them with detailed imagery, immersing yourself in the abundance and prosperity you desire.

Now, let's craft that script. Start with affirmations in the present tense, such as "I attract money effortlessly" or "I am deserving of financial prosperity." Keep it positive and empowering. Incorporate vibrant visualizations—picture-wise investments, unexpected windfalls, or the flourishing of your financial endeavors. Allow these mental images to evoke positive emotions, reinforcing your unwavering belief in your ability to manifest wealth.

Don't forget to address those limiting beliefs. If the specter of scarcity haunts your thoughts, weave statements like "I release all scarcity mindsets and welcome limitless financial opportunities into my life" into your script. Once your script is ready, record it and listen to it daily, especially in the morning and before bedtime when your subconscious is most receptive. Dedicate time to this practice, for consistency is your most formidable ally in reprogramming your subconscious mind for financial success. It is said it takes around 66 days to form a new habit. So try this every day for 66 days straight in your mornings & evenings before sleep because this is when your subconscious mind is most susceptible. If you miss a day, continue to the next day. (If you don't want to record your own, you can also always search for an "abundance self-hypnosis" on "YouTube" and play it in the morning and evening as well!) Check out hypnosis apps to get started!

Hypnosis Practice:

1. **Prepare Your Space**

   - Find a quiet, comfortable place where you won't be disturbed for at least 20–30 minutes.
   - Dim the lights or use candles to create a calming atmosphere.
   - Sit in a comfortable chair or lie down in a relaxed position.
   - Optional: Play soft, instrumental music or nature sounds to enhance relaxation.

2. **Set Your Intention**

   - Be clear about your goal for the session. For abundance, you might focus on:
   - Financial prosperity
   - Opportunities for growth
   - Gratitude for what you already have
   - Write your intention down or repeat it in your mind. Example: *"I am open to receiving abundance in all areas of my life."*

3. **Relax Your Body**

   - Close your eyes and take three deep breaths, inhaling deeply through your nose and exhaling slowly through your mouth.
   - Perform a progressive muscle relaxation:

1. Focus on your toes, tense them for a few seconds, then release.
2. Move to your feet, calves, thighs, and so on, up to your head.
3. Feel each area soften and relax as you release tension.

4.Enter a Hypnotic State

- Visualize descending a staircase or walking down a peaceful path, counting down from 10 to 1 as you imagine going deeper into relaxation.
- With each count, tell yourself, *"I am going deeper into relaxation."*
- Feel your body become heavier and your mind quieter.

5. Plant Positive Suggestions

- In this deeply relaxed state, affirm your abundance mindset. Speak to yourself in the present tense:
- *"I am worthy of abundance."*
- *"Opportunities flow to me effortlessly."*
- *"I attract wealth, health, and happiness with ease."*
- Visualize yourself living an abundant life. Imagine scenarios where you feel financially secure, surrounded by opportunities, and deeply fulfilled.

6.Anchor the Feeling

- While deeply immersed in this state, place your hand over your heart or make a small physical gesture, like pressing your thumb and forefinger together.
- Associate this gesture with the feeling of abundance and gratitude.

7.Counting Up

- When ready to return, count from 1 to 5, telling yourself with each number:
- "I am becoming more awake and energized."
- "I bring this feeling of abundance back with me."

8.Gently Open Your Eyes

- Take a deep breath, stretch if needed, and smile, knowing the seeds of abundance have been planted in your subconscious.

Visualization

Visualization is a dynamic technique that conjures vibrant mental landscapes of your dream financial life. It's not just idle daydreaming; it's a magnetic force that engages your subconscious mind, magnetizing your reality to effortlessly attract and manifest the wealth you visualize with your heart's desires.

One of the most potent strategies for manifesting money using your subconscious mind is visualization. By vividly imagining yourself already living your desired financial reality, you send powerful signals to your subconscious that align your thoughts, beliefs, and actions toward your goals. Visualize yourself enjoying the abundance you seek, feeling the emotions connected with financial prosperity. Let your subconscious absorb and embody this image into your being, making it your new reality. To manifest money by reprogramming your limiting beliefs in your subconscious mind, it is crucial to identify and address any negative or self-sabotaging thoughts that may be holding you back. Use affirmations and positive self-talk to challenge and replace limiting beliefs with empowering ones. Repetition is key; by consistently repeating positive affirmations, you gradually replace the old programming in your subconscious mind, paving the way for cultivating a transformed life.

Your subconscious mind, your trusty partner in this cosmic synergy, doesn't discern between real and imagined. As you consistently conjure these vivid mental images of financial triumph, it embarks on a frenzied mission to make those dreams a reality. Picture yourself as the mastermind and your subconscious as the eager accomplice, ceaselessly working to breathe life into your visions.

Practice 10-30 min:

1. **Creating a Relaxing Environment**: Begin by ensuring you're in a quiet, comfortable space where you won't be disturbed. This helps in reducing external distractions, making it easier to focus inwardly.
2. **Relaxation and Breathing Techniques**: Start with deep breathing exercises or a progressive muscle relaxation technique to induce a state of physical and mental relaxation. This step is crucial as it prepares the mind and body for a more receptive state.
3. **Focus and Concentration**: With your eyes closed concentrate on your senses, a specific sound, or even your own breathing. This helps in narrowing your awareness and increasing your susceptibility to suggestion.
4. **Positive and Specific Affirmations**: Once in a relaxed state, begin introducing positive affirmations related to abundance. These should be specific, positive, and in the present tense. For example, "I am capable of attracting wealth and success in my life."
5. **Visualization Technique**: Engage in vivid visualization. Picture yourself achieving your goals and experiencing abundance with great details. The more detailed and sensory-rich the visualization, the more effective it can be.
6. **Feelings**: Feel the feelings of your manifestations have already

happened!

7. **Receptive State for Suggestion**: In this state of deep relaxation and focused concentration, the mind becomes more open to suggestions. This is the time to reinforce your affirmations and visualizations about abundance.

8. **Regular Practice**: Consistency is key in self-hypnosis. Regular practice helps in reinforcing the new thought patterns and beliefs about abundance.

9. **Gradual Return to Full Awareness**: After completing your session, gradually bring yourself back to full consciousness. Avoid rushing out of the hypnotic state.

10. **Reflection and Adaptation**: Reflect on the experience and adjust your approach as needed for future sessions.

11. **Integrating into Daily Life**: Finally, try to integrate the positive affirmations and beliefs into your everyday life. This continuous reinforcement can help solidify these new patterns of thought.

Meditation

Practice the sacred art of meditation—a portal to realms beyond this dimension. Picture yourself in a serene sanctuary, where the world's clamor fades into silence, and you descend into a profound state of relaxation. Here, in this tranquil oasis, you unlock the gateway to your subconscious—a realm where limiting beliefs about money are replaced with empowering ones. Negativity fades into the background as you communicate with the Universe in your meditations. Look for flashes of visions, ideas, and messages from the Universe. Your subconscious is now your ally, believing wholeheartedly in your innate power to manifest abundance and prosperity.

Meditate as a daily ritual, a life-long journey for profound and lasting change. Once harnessed, the hidden power within your subconscious mind becomes the compass guiding your mindset away from scarcity and toward the boundless realm of abundance. It's an alchemy where each step ushers in remarkable shifts in your financial landscape.

Vibes

Now, let's veer into the mystical world of vibrational frequencies. Imagine your essence radiating a powerful resonance that beckons the Universe, summoning your desired riches. Maintaining a high vibrational frequency is the siren call that leads you toward financial prosperity.

Your subconscious mind, the maestro of your mind symphony, plays a pivotal role in this cosmic energy. It becomes your guiding star in visualizing and manifesting your financial dreams. As you paint the vivid canvas of your monetary aspirations, you send a crystal-clear message to the cosmos, aligning your vibrational frequency with the abundant cosmic frequencies. The result? A magnetic cosmic current that ushers the energy of money effortlessly into your life.

To keep this vibrational frequency soaring, you enlist two formidable allies: gratitude and positive thinking. Gratitude, the elixir of transformation, shifts your gaze from scarcity to boundless abundance. By honoring and celebrating the money you possess, you ignite a magnetic force that attracts more. Positive thinking, the empowering anthem, becomes your daily mantra, summoning positive experiences and opportunities that catalyze your financial transformation.

So, gear up for this riveting journey—a transformative quest through the realms of subconscious manifestation techniques through your vibrational frequencies. Get ready to embark on an abundant journey deep into the heart of transformation. This journey explores the magnetic forces of gratitude and the abundance mindset that power your vibrational frequencies, igniting your path toward financial prosperity. Developing an attitude of abundance and appreciation is crucial to attracting financial wealth. By focusing on what we already have and expressing gratitude for it, we emit positive energy that attracts more abundance into our lives.

Gratitude

The art of gratitude is a practice that involves acknowledging and wholeheartedly celebrating the blessings and abundance that grace your life. When you immerse yourself in gratitude, something magical happens. Your focus shifts away from the parched desert of scarcity and onto the lush landscape of abundance. It's a radical shift from a world of insufficiency to one brimming with plenty.

Here's where the marvel of the cosmic law of attraction takes center stage. This universal principle proclaims that like attracts like—an exquisite relation that plays out in the grand theater of our lives. Your thoughts and beliefs are magnetic forces, pulling in experiences that align with them. When you radiate gratitude for the money flowing through your life, you send a powerful signal to the universe. It's a declaration, a proclamation that you're ready and open to receive even more. This signal becomes a beacon, drawing in opportunities, insights, and resources to pave your path to financial abundance.

Having an abundant mindset is the core of cultivating abundant energy. Picture it as an unshakable belief that our world is a boundless reservoir of wealth and resources, with more than enough to go around, including your share. It starkly contrasts the scarcity mindset, which whispers tales of a limited pool of riches and suggests that others' success somehow dims your financial prospects. As you embrace the abundance mindset, you don a new pair of glasses through which you see life. Suddenly, the world transforms; every challenge becomes an opportunity, and every obstacle a stepping stone. This mindset becomes your guiding light, propelling you toward your financial goals and swinging the gates wide to the abundance that eagerly awaits your arrival.

But here's the captivating part—unlocking the full wonders of gratitude and the abundant mindset involves embarking on a profound quest. It's about rewriting the script of your subconscious, freeing it from the clutches of limiting beliefs woven into your story. These beliefs often trace their roots to the canvas of your early experiences, societal conditioning, or past financial hurdles. But hypnosis, meditation, and visualization tools for subconscious reprogramming are your allies in this quest. Within this mystical realm, you journey into the depths of your mind, unveiling and releasing these limiting beliefs individually. In their place, you plant the seeds of empowering beliefs that champion your journey toward financial success.

This alchemizing journey grants you access to the extraordinary power of your subconscious mind—a realm that quietly engineers 95% of your thoughts, actions, and behaviors. As you rewire your subconscious thoughts, you set the stage for a harmonious symphony that propels you toward financial abundance. It's a transformative voyage where the currents of gratitude and the sails of an abundant mindset carry you forward into uncharted waters, teeming with the treasures of prosperity.

In the world we've grown up in, it's been drilled into our heads that hard work and a degree are the keys to financial success. But there's a whole universe of possibilities swirling within us, where intuition becomes our guiding star—a star that leads us to choices and actions that lead to our divine purpose and attract abundance!

Daily Rituals: Morning & Evening Routines

1. Gratitude Practice: Begin each day by expressing gratitude for the abundance in your life. Focus on the money you have, the opportunities that come your way, and the resources available to you. By appreciating what you already have, you create a positive vibration that attracts more abundance into your life.

2. Money Mantras: Develop a set of money mantras you can recite daily. For example, "Money flows to me easily and effortlessly," or "I am open and receptive to all forms of wealth." Repeat these mantras whenever you think negatively about money or need inspiration throughout your day.

3. Scripting: Write your desires as if they have already happened 1-3 pages. For example, instead of saying, "I will have a successful career," write, "I have a thriving and fulfilling career." This helps shift your mindset into believing your desires are already a reality. The more specific and detailed you can be in your script, the better. Describe how you feel, what you see, who is with you, and any other sensory details that make your manifestation more real. This specificity helps to create a clear picture in your mind.

4. Meditate: Find a quiet and comfortable place to meditate. This could be a designated corner of your home or a peaceful outdoor spot. Setting up this sacred space helps create a conducive environment for meditation. Start the meditation by relaxing your body and mind. Focus on breathing, taking slow, deep breaths, inhaling positive energy, and exhaling negative thoughts. Emphasize the importance of feeling the emotions associated with abundance during the meditation. Feel the joy, gratitude, and excitement as if you already have the abundance in your life.

5. Visualization: Take a few minutes daily to visualize yourself living a prosperous life. Imagine yourself enjoying the luxuries you desire, seeing yourself effortlessly manifest large sums of money, and feeling the emotions of financial freedom. Visualization connects you with the energy of abundance and helps you manifest it into reality. Lastly, any attachments you hold on to the outcome should be released. Visualization is about aligning with the energy of abundance rather than chasing it. Trust that the universe will bring abundance in the right way and time.

6. Financial Education: Expand your knowledge about money, investments, and financial literacy. Read books, take courses, or listen to podcasts that provide valuable insight into building wealth. Educating yourself about money enhances your financial IQ and strengthens your money mindset.

Remember, the key is regular daily practice, as it is most effective when done consistently. Set aside dedicated time each day for your practice. After any practice, take a moment to reflect on any insights or ideas that may have arisen during the session. Take inspired action towards any ideas that may have sprouted, as action is essential to manifesting abundance.

Incorporating these daily practices into your life will nurture and strengthen your money mindset. Remember that consistency is key when it comes to reprogramming your subconscious mind. With time, patience, and dedication, you will begin to witness the transformation of your financial reality as you manifest abundance with intention.

4

What You Focus On Manifests

The Reticular Activating System (RAS) is the part of your brain that discerns which information receives the VIP access pass to your awareness and what gets relegated to the shadows. It tirelessly scans the terrain of your existence, eager to spotlight the most pertinent signals that align with your prevailing thoughts.

Dominant thoughts, those steadfast sentinels of your mental realm, are the blueprints that construct your reality, both consciously and subconsciously. While the RAS is primarily a conductor of your alertness and focus steered by your dominant thoughts, it affects your perception and cognitive processes.

Your RAS plays a crucial role in shaping your view of the world. Picture it as a selective filter, sifting through the sensory clutter of your environment to admit only what resonates with your primary dominant thoughts. This filtering system results from how your focused attention influences the RAS. By consistently concentrating on particular thoughts, goals, or aspirations, you signal to your RAS what matters most to you. Consequently, this guides your attention and awareness to align with those thoughts, drawing you to opportunities, individuals, and situations that fit seamlessly with your dominant thoughts and desires.

Your dominant thoughts, those enduring ideas that inhabit your conscious and subconscious, command the attention of your RAS. The adage 'what you focus on is what you manifest' relates directly to the Reticular Activating System. Your conscious attention and focus shape how your brain filters and interprets the world's stimuli. By persistently directing your thoughts towards positivity, goals, and aspirations, you can effectively tune your RAS to be more receptive to opportunities and experiences that resonate with your desired outcomes in life.

For example, Imagine you are aspiring to start your own business. If you constantly think about your business goals, strategies, and success, your RAS will become more attuned to information and opportunities related to your business. You might notice networking events, business resources, or potential partners you previously overlooked. This heightened awareness and focus on your goals can increase the likelihood of manifesting your business aspirations.

Your RAS meticulously selects which thoughts should be prominently on your mind while relegating others to the dusty storage room. When a specific thought dominates your mental stage, the RAS agrees, spotlighting information bolsters that thought. This selective attention further amplifies and reinforces your dominant thoughts.

How the Mind Shapes Reality

Due to the Reticular Activating System (RAS), confirmation bias and self-fulfilling prophecies form a feedback loop that shapes how we perceive the world and molds the reality we experience. This explains how **our perception of reality doesn't just reflect the world—it actively shapes it.** When we understand how this cause-and-effect works, we can intentionally program our minds to align our thoughts and beliefs to work for our benefit.

The RAS: The Brain's Precision Filter

At the foundation of this process lies the Reticular Activating System, a neural network nestled in the brainstem. The RAS is like the brain's control tower, tasked with filtering the overwhelming sensory input we encounter every second. From 40 million bits of information, the RAS selects the 40 most relevant to our conscious awareness.

But the RAS doesn't choose what's relevant on its own. It takes its cues from us—our beliefs, desires, and expectations. This explains why that model seems to appear on every street after we decide to buy a particular car. The RAS, attuned to what we've flagged as necessary, brings it into focus.

Yet, this exact mechanism can work against us. If we believe we're incapable of success, the RAS will dutifully highlight every stumble and misstep, reinforcing the narrative we hold about ourselves. It doesn't question whether our beliefs are empowering or limiting—it simply delivers what we prioritize.

Confirmation Bias: The Belief Amplifier

Once the RAS decides what information reaches our conscious mind, confirmation bias takes over. This cognitive process ensures we notice, remember, and emphasize evidence supporting our existing beliefs while dismissing or downplaying anything challenging.

This creates a self-reinforcing loop. Someone who believes they're "terrible with money" will notice and give importance to every financial mistake they've made while ignoring moments of savvy decision-making. Conversely, someone who sees themselves as resilient will vividly recall their triumphs over adversity while minimizing their struggles. This illustrates confirmation bias. Your cognitive system is wired to pursue and interpret information that aligns with your preexisting beliefs, while contradictory evidence is often overlooked. The RAS is instrumental in this process, selectively highlighting ideas that align with your dominant thoughts.

Confirmation bias filters reality, creating a version of the world where our beliefs seem irrefutably authentic. Confirmation bias seeks and collects evidence to prove our beliefs correct, reinforcing the belief to be stronger. So be careful what you choose to believe and how strongly you believe it because it will manifest and create your reality!

Our beliefs don't just shape how we *see* the world—they sculpt how we *experience* it. Like a river carving its path through stone, our convictions quietly yet powerfully mold the landscapes of our lives. Our beliefs are powerful as we live according to them, such as religion.

History shows us repeatedly how what we once held as unshakable truth often crumbles under the weight of discoveries. Once upon a time, in the mid-20th century, doctors were plastered all over cigarette ads, endorsing them and suggesting health benefits. Flash forward a few decades, and we now understand the devastating links to cancer from smoking. Think of someone's grandparents who may stick to this belief and never change to belief in the new research. This dramatic reversal is a powerful reminder that our current "certainties" may look very different through tomorrow's lens.

In our modern information landscape, we face an even more significant challenge. Research can be shaped by biases with personal motives, and now fake news is generated from artificial intelligence. This doesn't mean we should abandon our trust in science—instead, it calls us to develop a more sophisticated investigation with truth. It means we need to sharpen our swords of discernment and become warriors for truth instead of passive sponges for every new headline.

It's about striking that sweet balance between staying open-minded and knowing when to raise an eyebrow. This means diving into evidence like a truth detective, recognizing that new information may challenge our beliefs, and staying humble enough to admit when you're wrong. It also means embracing the idea that truth can sometimes unreveal itself over a long period of time, like getting your films developed for disposable cameras—waiting for those wedding photos feels like years versus having them taken from your iPhone!

Think of your belief system not as a fortress made of concrete but as a living, breathing garden. Some ideas will sprout and bloom into life-changing revelations. Others will wither and die under the glaring sun of new evidence.

Be careful what you believe as it will manifest into your reality. Be like water, open and flexible in your beliefs. Truth can change, as exemplified in history. Everything in life constantly changes, including facts we believe are valid. Discern what is true carefully, but be open to what could be true and what is the truth. Imagine yourself in your 60s, perhaps as a grandparent. Will you resist being confined by the rigid mindset of "this is how it has always been, and always will be," or will you embrace change, evolving alongside the rapid advancements of the digital age?

Self-Fulfilling Prophecies: The Feedback Loop of Reality Creation

When filtered perceptions and amplified beliefs drive behavior, they create self-fulfilling prophecies. These are loops where our actions, driven by our internal narratives, generate outcomes that validate those narratives.

Imagine an entrepreneur who doubts their ability to succeed. Their RAS highlights every obstacle, and their confirmation bias amplifies every misstep. These beliefs may lead to cautious or hesitant actions, which result in missed opportunities, further reinforcing their initial doubts.

Now consider the opposite: an entrepreneur who trusts in their ability to innovate. Their RAS can spot patterns, trends, and opportunities others might miss. Their confirmation bias highlights evidence of progress, strengthening their confidence. This belief fuels bold action, producing outcomes that affirm their sense of capability.

The loop perpetuates in both cases, turning beliefs into tangible reality.

Your Emotions: The Hidden Engineers of Your Reality

Emotions are another key indicator. When a thought carries emotional weight, it carries a more substantial energetic charge in your mental landscape, influencing your perception of the world. If your thoughts are perpetually clouded by worry or anxiety, your RAS will cast a shadow over even the brightest opportunities. Your emotions are far more than temporary sensations; they fuel your actions. Every thought and feeling you experience carries an energetic charge, subtly influencing how you perceive the world and what you allow into your conscious awareness. This profound connection between emotion and perception is the key to unlocking the incredible power within your brain. Understanding your emotions' profound role in shaping your mental processes, including the Reticular Activating System (RAS), confirmation bias, and self-fulfilling prophecies, allows you to harness them for personal growth and success.

The RAS, a key gatekeeper in your brain, doesn't merely filter out irrelevant information—it selectively prioritizes what matters to you most. And the emotional weight behind your thoughts is what determines what matters. When a thought carries significant emotional energy, whether that emotion is joy, fear, excitement, or anxiety, it activates your RAS and shapes what you see. If you're filled with enthusiasm and gratitude, your RAS becomes attuned to uplifting signals. Opportunities appear, encouraging interactions to materialize, and moments of beauty become undeniable. However, when fear or worry clouds your mind, the RAS shifts focus, filtering the world through a lens of caution and potential threat. In this state, even promising situations can seem risky or unattainable. The stronger the emotional resonance behind a thought, the greater its influence on your perception, making it clear that your emotional state doesn't just color your experience—it creates it.

Confirmation bias reinforces your emotional perspective once the RAS has filtered the information. Your brain is naturally inclined to search for evidence that confirms what you already believe, and when those beliefs are intertwined with intense emotions, confirmation bias fuels your perception. If you're feeling confident, your brain will gather all the evidence supporting your belief in your success. The compliments you receive, the small victories you experience, and even the way things seem to flow effortlessly prove that you're on the right path. But if you're gripped by doubt or fear, your confirmation bias will deliver a steady stream of "proof" that your worries are justified, pointing out every misstep and every moment of uncertainty. In either case, your emotions guide what your brain chooses to highlight, ensuring that your perception of reality always aligns with how you feel.

As this emotional energy flows through your perception, it doesn't just stay in the mental realm—it actively shapes your actions. How you feel directly influences how you engage with the world around you, and the results of those actions create a self-reinforcing loop. When you feel confident and motivated, your actions are bold, and your energy draws opportunities. Your RAS picks up on these moments, and your confirmation bias validates your belief in your capabilities. Success breeds more success, and this cycle continues, elevating you toward your goals. However, when you feel anxious or defeated, your actions can become hesitant, cautious, and disengaged. Your RAS focuses on potential threats, and confirmation bias amplifies the belief that failure is imminent. This creates an environment where missed opportunities and setbacks only confirm the negative narrative in your mind. The loop continues, reinforcing the belief that things will never improve.

This process, while automatic, isn't inevitable. When you realize that your emotions are not merely reactions to external events but the powerful forces that shape your internal world, you gain the ability to transform your reality. You are not a passive observer of your life; you are the creator. By intentionally cultivating the emotions that serve you—those that align with your vision and goals—you shift the entire mechanism of your mind in your favor. When you actively focus on gratitude, joy, and excitement, your RAS becomes finely tuned to notice opportunities, solutions, and paths forward. Your confirmation bias will seek evidence to reinforce your belief in your success, and your actions will naturally align with your desired outcome.

Your emotions are not just fleeting moments of feeling—they are the energy that fuels the narrative of your life. The world around you has endless potential, but your emotional state determines whether or not you will notice it. Once you understand how emotions guide your RAS, confirmation bias, and self-fulfilling prophecies, you realize that your ability to shape your life is in your hands. When you consciously cultivate the right emotional energy, you stop reacting to life's circumstances and create experiences reflecting your most authentic desires. Your emotions are not just feelings—they are the compass that directs you toward your every decision, guiding you toward the future you choose to manifest.

The Power of Mindset

The feedback loop formed by the RAS, confirmation bias, and self-fulfilling prophecies isn't inherently good or bad—it simply reflects the beliefs we feed it. This is why two people can encounter identical situations and draw completely different conclusions. A seasoned trader views a market downturn as a moment to seize opportunities; a novice sees only loss and panic. The difference lies not in external circumstances, but in the mental framework, each brings to the experience.

The implications are profound. Our perception of reality doesn't passively mirror the world—it actively sculpts it. By shifting the beliefs that guide the RAS and feed our biases, we can change how we engage with challenges, opportunities, and success.

Far from being a mystical phenomenon, the ability to "manifest" success is rooted in the mechanics of the brain. The RAS filters the world through the lens of our goals. Confirmation bias ensures that evidence aligns with our beliefs. Self-fulfilling prophecies create actions and outcomes that reinforce those beliefs. This feedback loop is the foundation of human potential and operates whether we're aware of it or not.

The question isn't whether this system will shape our reality—it's **how**. When we consciously align our thoughts, beliefs, and focus with the desired outcomes, we're not just passively observing life but actively constructing it. This is the intersection where neuroscience meets empowerment, offering us the tools to transform our perceptions and possibilities. Understanding how the mind shapes reality, we can construct our reality by understanding the workings of the mind through the RAS, starting with our beliefs.

Now, let's pivot to the grand reveal: your RAS can be your partner in prosperity. When you foster dominant thoughts of abundance, success, and financial well-being, you awaken the dormant potential of life's possibilities. With your thoughts steeped in prosperity, your RAS transforms into a diligent assistant armed with a refined filter that sifts the world in search of previously obscured opportunities, connections, and resources. It's as if the universe conspires to align with your financial ambitions. The key to this transformation lies in your thoughts—dominant thoughts of abundance catalyze this paradigm shift.

Picture the RAS as your trusted gatekeeper, selectively ushering sensory input into the grand theater of your conscious mind. It meticulously sifts out the extraneous and ushers forth only the most aligned information that harmonizes with your dominant musings. If a particular notion wields dominion over your mental landscape, the RAS may shine a spotlight on stimuli that affirm and resonate with that thought. This laser-focused attention serves to fortify and amplify your dominant thoughts.

Your RAS is more than a filter; it's a goal-seeking mechanism, a silent evidence gatherer in your pursuit of financial success. When abundance dominates your thoughts, your RAS embarks on a relentless quest for information, strategies, and pathways leading to your financial aspirations. The Reticular Activating System (RAS) is like a laser beam of attention in our minds. Just as a laser beam can precisely focus on a specific point, the RAS sharpens our awareness to concentrate on essential information amidst the vast sea of stimuli in our daily lives. It filters out the noise, highlighting what truly matters, much like a laser's intense, directed light pierces through the darkness toward its target.

As your RAS serves up abundant related stimuli to your conscious awareness, you'll enter a positive feedback loop. Success begets more success, and your dominant thoughts of prosperity strengthen with each triumph, propelling you forward with an accelerating momentum.

By consciously guiding your thoughts towards abundance and training your RAS to be your unwavering ally, you'll discover that the path to financial success is an infinitely rewarding journey. So, let the RAS be your loyal Dachshund in manifesting abundance.

Not to be overlooked, dominant thoughts harbor potent emotions. Imagine the stress and anxiety that accompany the relentless contemplation of a thorny predicament. These emotional undercurrents serve as a compass that guides the RAS. Thoughts dripping with emotion commandeer your attention and mold your perception of the world's tableau.

Now, consider that your dominant thoughts can be tethered to your goals and aspirations. When a clear, unwavering goal takes root in your consciousness, the RAS becomes your faithful ally. It becomes your "goal-seeking mechanism." This guardian actively seeks out fragments of wisdom, strategies, and pathways leading to financial prosperity. It transforms into a silent partner, whispering directions to your eager soul.

Dominant thoughts are the architects of your destiny, designing the blueprint for your actions, choices, and outlook. Nurturing thoughts of abundance and fiscal well-being is imperative to unlocking the vaults of financial success.

Here's the roadmap: embrace thoughts saturated with abundance and watch your RAS metamorphose into a gold-mining filter. It will unearth opportunities, forge connections, and unveil resources previously eluded your notice. This heightened perception will set you on a course guided by your financial aspirations.

Behold the RAS, your steadfast companion in the pursuit of greatness. As your dominant thoughts embrace prosperity, this trusty sight-hunting dog is like a loyal Dachshund on a quest. It searches for knowledge, strategies, and routes that pave the way to financial triumph. Your RAS becomes your assistant in steering you toward your ambitions.

With your RAS as the herald of abundance, witness the positive feedback loops. Experience the principle of "what you seek, you will find." Each achievement bolsters your dominion over thoughts of abundance, propelling you closer to your financial dreams.

In summation, the nexus between your dominant thoughts and the Reticular Activating System is a potent force, an alliance that can direct your financial destiny. By consciously steering your thoughts toward abundance and training your RAS to be your ally, you will find that the road to financial abundance becomes attainable with a collaboration with the power of your mind.

5

Positive Mind

The realm of abundance isn't just about the zeros in your bank account; it's about the abundance of everything in life. You might have primarily thought of tangible cash initially, but think of abundance in every other way. You might think you don't have enough if all your focus is on the numbers in your bank account. The truth is abundance is everywhere because abundance is as natural as nature. Look around you. Nature itself is the perfect example of unlimited abundance. Fruit trees bear fruit effortlessly, season after season, without checking bank accounts. The oceans stretch far beyond what the eye can see, their waves continuously lapping against the shore, abundant and never-ending. Flowers bloom, rivers flow, and the air is fresh and free—there is no scarcity in nature, only perpetual renewal and supply.

If the universe provides so abundantly in nature, why do we doubt its ability to provide for us? Why do we operate from a mindset of lack when we are surrounded by evidence that life is endlessly giving? The truth is that abundance is our birthright. It is natural. It is everywhere. But we must shift our focus to recognize it.

Nature is abundance, and if you focus on your billing statements, you exile all the abundant beauty of what life has to offer. Take a moment to step away from obsessing about money and getting rich quickly and shift to the perspective of how you are already abundant in many ways, starting with the fact that you are a living miracle. The probability of your exact existence, with your unique DNA, personality, and experiences, is infinitesimally small—yet here you are. That alone is evidence of an abundant universe that has conspired to create you.

Now, consider the relationships in your life. The love of friends, family, and even the kindness of strangers is an abundance of connection. The knowledge you have acquired, the experiences that have shaped you, and the skills you have developed are all forms of wealth that cannot be measured in currency. So many forms of abundance cannot be counted through paper or coin currency. You can be abundant with your kindness, energy, spirit, and service.

You have an abundance of opportunities every single day. You have access to information, to creativity, to inspiration. The possibilities for growth, joy, and contribution are endless. When you shift your focus away from what you perceive as missing and instead embrace the wealth of life's offerings, you invite more abundance into your reality.

Life is about the richness of your experiences, the strength of your relationships, your health, and your overall quality of life. Abundance is a state of being. It sprouts from the seeds of your positive mindset, nurturing every aspect of your life and flourishing into prosperity. There is an undeniable connection between abundance and a positive mind, unveiling how shifting your perspective can unlock your desired abundance. Let's begin by reimagining what abundance truly means. We often focus solely on material possessions or financial gains when we think of abundance. But true abundance extends far beyond these tangible measures. It encompasses the richness of your inner well of spirit, your life experiences, the warmth and depth of your relationships, the vitality of your health, and the joy you find in each moment. A life filled with positive experiences, meaningful connections, and vibrant health is a life of abundance and a soulful life, a life of abundance in its purest form.

A positive mind is the start of opening the gates to abundance and its abundance in all forms. Imagine a mindset that anticipates joy, success, and beautiful outcomes in every situation and area of your life. That's the power of positivity: it transforms ordinary moments into extraordinary experiences, attracting miracles naturally. Positivity is not merely an individual pursuit but an energetic force extending far beyond you. A mind trained to expect goodness naturally fosters creativity, possibilities, resilience, and openness, drawing in people and opportunities that align with its positive frequency.

Imagine a consciousness so finely tuned to the frequency of positivity, joy, and limitless possibility that every moment radiates potential. This is the power of genuine positivity and abundance through the art of alchemy—not just fleeting optimism but an unwavering inner state that transmutes the mundane into the extraordinary. Like an alchemist turning lead into gold, your thoughts can shape reality, inviting miracles and turning challenges into stepping stones toward an adventurous journey to greatness. A positive mindset does not shield you from hardship but elevates your response. Every obstacle carries the blueprint of its solution, every setback is a setup for a more significant comeback, and every moment of adversity refines your vision. It gives you the power to be the creator at every moment; you can conjure positive spirits for creative possibilities to manifest at any moment.

Your mind is a fertile garden, and every thought is a seed. Nurture thoughts of possibility, positivity, and abundance, and your inner landscape will blossom into a field of infinite potential. Each day is an invitation to weed out doubt and plant fresh seeds of optimism. Joy is a catalyst, a magnetic force that attracts abundance effortlessly.

When you enthusiastically move through life, you become irresistible—drawing in opportunities, deepening connections, and aligning with serendipitous breakthroughs. This is the natural consequence of being positive for others who want to collaborate with you, which will support and uplift your life. People are compelled to be part of your vision when you radiate authentic positivity. They see your light and want to walk alongside you. The universe mirrors your internal state—what you give out, you receive.

Neuroplasticity

Through the science of neuroplasticity, you can rewire your neural pathways to cultivate an abundance mindset. Our brains are marvelously malleable, possessing a quality known as neuroplasticity. This means we can change our thought patterns, create new neural pathways, and favor positivity over negativity. Neuroplasticity is like having a reset button for your mind, allowing you to reshape your thinking patterns and emotional responses consciously. With neuroplasticity, we can harness and cultivate the mindset of abundance, which we need to attract abundance into our lives through positive thinking.

Neuroplasticity is your brain's ability to reorganize itself by forming new neural connections throughout life. Think of your thoughts as water flowing down a hillside. Over time, they create deeper grooves, making it easier for water to follow these established paths. Similarly, your thought patterns create neural pathways that become stronger with repetition.

To understand this concept better, imagine your brain as a sprawling city. The streets are neural pathways, the traffic signals are synapses, and the vehicles represent the flow of information. The most frequently traveled paths become highways—wider, faster, and more efficient. Our habitual thoughts and attitudes carve the neural landscapes of our brains, creating well-worn pathways that guide our responses to the world.

The revolutionary insight is this: you're not stuck with the mental pathways you've historically created. Through conscious effort and specific practices, you can carve new channels for your thoughts to flow, literally restructuring your brain to support an abundance mindset. Like the potter's clay or the artist's canvas, your neural architecture is waiting to be shaped by conscious intention's gentle but persistent hand.

When you habitually think of thoughts of scarcity and limitation, you strengthen neural pathways associated with fear, lack, and pessimism. This creates a self-reinforcing cycle in which your amygdala—the brain's fear center—becomes more reactive, triggering the release of stress hormones like cortisol more frequently. Your brain becomes primed to notice threats and limitations, and your decision-making abilities become compromised under stress.

Consider how the mind creates its limitations. When you believe in scarcity, your brain's fear center—the amygdala—becomes like an overprotective guardian, casting shadows of doubt and limitation across your consciousness. This is not always the complete truth; it is simply a pattern, a habit of neural firing that has been reinforced through unconscious repetition.

In the depths of your brain, a remarkable system called the Reticular Activating System (RAS) acts as a filter for reality itself. When programmed with scarcity, it dutifully presents evidence of lack and limitation. But here lies the miracle: when illuminated by abundance consciousness, this same system becomes a magnetic force for opportunity and possibility.

Now, think about the thoughts that you regularly entertain. If you're constantly thinking, "I'm terrible with money," or "I'll never be rich," you're essentially paving superhighways of negativity toward money in your mind. The more you reinforce these beliefs, the more they become ingrained. These thought patterns influence your behaviors to block money, limit your ability to see opportunities and cultivate the mindset of abundance that leads to wealth.

The good news is that you can consciously redirect these neural pathways. The process begins with neural pruning: when you stop reinforcing negative thought patterns, these neural pathways weaken, just as unused trails become overgrown. Your brain creates new synaptic connections supporting these thought patterns as you practice positive thinking. These new pathways become insulated with myelin, making them stronger and more efficient. Eventually, positive thinking becomes your brain's default mode, requiring less conscious effort.

The transformation begins with a single sacred act: the conscious direction of attention. Just as the sun's rays, when focused through a lens, can ignite a flame, your focused attention can ignite new neural pathways of abundance. What modern neuroscience is discovering aligns perfectly with quantum physics: consciousness shapes reality. Your brain is not just responding to the world; it is actively creating your experience. When you change your neural patterns, you change how your consciousness interacts with the quantum field of infinite possibility.

Neuroplasticity gives us the ability to build new roads of thought patterns. We can consciously create new neural pathways promoting positivity, abundance, and success. By shifting our thoughts about money and abundance, we can rewire our brains for prosperity. For example, instead of thinking, "Money is the root of all evil," replace that with, "Money is a tool for good." Instead of believing, "I'll never be rich," switch to "Wealth is within my reach." These simple shifts aren't just positive affirmations; they're cognitive restructurings that lay the foundation for new, empowering dominant thought patterns that create your life.

When you understand how neuroplasticity works, manifestation becomes more practical. Your Reticular Activating System (RAS) filters information based on your focus. When you prime it for abundance, you notice more opportunities in your environment. This isn't a coincidence—it's neuroscience in action.

Positive thinking releases dopamine and serotonin, improving your decision-making abilities, creative problem-solving skills, social connections, and resilience. As your neural pathways change, your behaviors naturally align with abundance thinking, creating real-world results.

Think of your brain as a sophisticated computer running an outdated program of scarcity. Through neuroplasticity, you can install and strengthen a new abundance operating system. Each positive thought, grateful moment, and abundance visualization creates new neural pathways that support your desired reality.

Your brain's plasticity is not just a biological fact—it is a gateway to personal enlightenment. By directing your attention in a conscious way, regularly communion with abundance consciousness, and persistently choosing to align with possibility rather than limitation, you are not just changing your mind; you are evolving your very being.

The journey of rewiring your brain for abundance begins with daily practice. Each morning, as you wake, take time to visualize scenarios of abundance in your life. This isn't mere daydreaming—you're actively creating new neural pathways. Throughout your day, when you catch yourself in scarcity thinking, pause. Take three deep breaths. Let your mind drift to moments of gratitude, allowing your brain to forge new connections associated with abundance.

Your physical environment plays a crucial role in this rewiring process. Consider your space an external reflection of your internal abundance. Create an environment that reminds you of plenty, possibility, and growth. Surround yourself with people who embody the abundance mindset you're cultivating, as their neural patterns will influence yours through the mirror neuron system.

The power to rewire your brain for abundance lies in your moment-to-moment choices about where to direct your attention and energy. Whenever you focus on abundance rather than scarcity, you strengthen these new neural pathways. You build a more resilient abundance network in your brain whenever you practice gratitude instead of complaint.

If you feel lost about how to start your positive thinking journey, start with gratitude. Each time you choose to dwell in gratitude, your brain releases a cascade of neurochemicals—dopamine, serotonin, and oxytocin—that not only feel magnificent but literally reshape your neural architecture. Each time you visualize abundance with full sensory engagement, you're not just daydreaming but engineering new neural networks that automatically seek and create abundance in your life.

One of the most powerful ways to experience abundance is through gratitude. Gratitude is the practice of recognizing and appreciating what you already have, and in doing so, you amplify its presence in your life. When you are grateful, you tell the universe, "I recognize the abundance all around me, and I am open to receiving more."

Instead of fixating on what is absent, focus on what is overflowing. Feel the sun's warmth on your skin, the taste of your favorite meal, and the laughter of a loved one. These are riches beyond measure. When you cultivate gratitude, you shift your vibration from scarcity to sufficiency and from sufficiency to overflow.

To truly embody abundance, begin living as though you are already wealthy—not necessarily in material terms, but in spirit. Walk with confidence, knowing that life is constantly providing for you. Give generously, knowing that there is always more to receive. Celebrate others' successes, understanding that their abundance does not diminish yours.

The realm of abundance is not where you arrive when you reach a particular financial milestone. It is a mindset you cultivate, a way of living that acknowledges the limitless nature of the universe. You will align your energy with the Source of the Universe, where limitless abundance originates. And when you truly embrace this truth, financial wealth often follows—not as a desperate pursuit, but as a natural byproduct of an abundant energy exuding from your inner well-being.

You are already abundant. You are already rich in ways that transcend money. The more you recognize and embrace this, the more you witness abundance expanding in every area of your life. Step into the realm of abundance, and watch how life unfolds in ways more magnificent than you ever imagined by aligning and tuning into the Source of all things in the Universe.

Regular meditation focused on abundance accelerates this rewiring process. As you sit in quiet contemplation, visualizing your abundant life, you're not just relaxing but actively restructuring your neural networks. This practice and conscious attention to your thoughts throughout the day create a powerful foundation for transformation.

Cognitive psychology affirms what visionaries have long understood: expectation molds experience. When you anticipate positive outcomes, your brain primes to recognize and act upon opportunities that reinforce your belief. It's as though you activate a filter that reveals hidden pathways to success, solutions in moments of adversity, and unseen doors waiting to be opened. This isn't about denying life's difficulties— it's about maintaining an unshakable confidence that every experience holds a seed of lessons for growth.

As you walk this path of conscious neural evolution, remember that each moment presents a choice: to reinforce the old patterns of scarcity or to illuminate new pathways of abundance. This is not about denying challenges but transcending the limited perspective that created them.

Positivity is not a passive trait; it is a practice. Each morning, set an intention to uncover joy, opportunity, and wisdom in every encounter. When faced with difficulty, ask yourself: What gift is hidden in this moment? What unseen opportunity lies within this challenge?

The Power of Positive Affirmations

As you work through these techniques, positive affirmations can play a vital role in reinforcing your new mindset. Affirmations are simple, declarative statements that align your thoughts with the abundance you seek. They remind you of the truth you want to embody and reinforce your commitment to change.

For example, start each day by repeating affirmations like:

- "I am worthy of wealth and success."
- "Abundance flows to me effortlessly."
- "I am a magnet for positive opportunities."
- "Every day, I attract more wealth and happiness."

When practiced consistently, affirmations help retrain your brain to favor positive thoughts and beliefs. Over time, they will become second nature, ingraining a mindset of abundance and success that supports all aspects of your life, not just your finances.

The ultimate goal is not just to think positively but to *be in a state of positivity*—to embody it so thoroughly that it becomes your essence. When this happens, you no longer need to force optimism; it flows effortlessly, attracting abundance as naturally as the sun draws flowers toward its light.

Like a lighthouse piercing through the fog, your inner radiance becomes a guiding force, pulling in opportunities, relationships, and resources that align with your highest potential. You do not chase abundance—it flows to you effortlessly because you are in harmony with its vibration.

Pause for a moment and consider: What if you embraced this way of being full? What possibilities might reveal themselves? What relationships might deepen? What long-held dreams might suddenly feel within reach?

The gateway to limitless abundance stands before you; the key is in your hands. Each thought of joy, each expectation of success, and each moment of deep gratitude opens the door wider, allowing the universe to bless you.

Remember: You need not strive for abundance—it is yours. It is your birthright, waiting to be uncovered through empowered perception.

Will you accept this invitation to transform your world? Choose now to see the extraordinary within the ordinary, and watch as the miraculous unfolds before your very eyes.

Abundance Begins from Within

The path to abundance begins in the mind. By cultivating a positive mindset, you open the door to abundance in every area of your life. Whether it's health, relationships, career, or finances, the thoughts you entertain can shape your reality. Neuroplasticity allows you to rewire your brain, creating new pathways that favor positivity and prosperity.

Remember that this process of neural rewiring is ongoing. Your brain changes throughout life, constantly adapting to your thoughts and experiences. Each day presents countless opportunities to strengthen positive neural networks and weaken limiting ones. The key lies in consistent practice and patient persistence.

The next chapter of your life begins with the following thought you choose to nurture. Make it one of abundance. The next time you step into the golden landscape of creating your mindset of abundance, remember that your mind is the fertile soil from which your wealth grows. By nurturing positive thoughts and cultivating an attitude of possibility, you can manifest the abundance already waiting for you.

Each new thought of abundance sends ripples through the quantum field. Each moment of gratitude reshapes your neural architecture. Each choice to align with possibility opens new pathways in the infinite garden of your mind.

The question is not whether you can transform—transformation is your natural state. The question is: will you consciously participate in your evolution? Will you step into the role of divine creator in the garden of your consciousness?

Your brain is waiting for you to take charge and to be rewired. The science is clear: you can transform your neural pathways to support an abundance mindset through conscious effort and consistent practice. As you close this chapter, consider this: what thoughts will you choose to focus on today? How will you direct your brain's remarkable plasticity toward creating the abundant life you desire?

6

Self-Worth

Your relationship with money is a mirror reflecting the depths of your self-worth. At its core, financial success is not merely about hard work, it's about the beliefs you carry about yourself. When self-worth is low, it quietly erodes your ability to receive abundance, whispering falsehoods of inadequacy that keep prosperity away. Many of us unknowingly carry limiting beliefs like heavy anchors, preventing the natural flow of money into our lives.

Deep within the chambers of our subconscious mind lie long-ago-planted beliefs about our worthiness. Like invisible threads, these beliefs weave through every financial decision we make, every opportunity we embrace or reject, and every dollar we allow ourselves to receive or push away. Some of us carry these beliefs like ancient stones in our pockets, so familiar that we've forgotten they're there, yet they weigh us down with every step.

But here's the truth: You are inherently worthy of abundance. The key to unlocking financial abundance is recognizing and honoring your unique gifts, talents, and contributions. When deeply believing in your value, you radiate powerful energy that effortlessly attracts opportunities, resources, and success. True wealth sprouts from a strong sense of self-worth—from scarcity to sufficiency and doubt to confidence. When you step into your worth, abundance will no longer be something you chase; it will be something you naturally attract.

Imagine that you are a flower growing in a vast garden. Would you question your right to receive sunlight and nutrients from the soil? Would you apologize for taking up space or blooming in your full glory? Of course not. Yet how often do we question our right to receive abundance, shine in our full brilliance, and receive the fruits of our labor?

Like a diamond buried deep within the earth, its value is intrinsic, unchangeable, and eternal. You are that diamond. Your worth isn't determined by your bank account, achievements, or others' opinions. It is fundamental to your existence, a truth written in the very fabric of your soul. Yet how many of us live like diamonds that have forgotten their worth, believing instead that we are mere pebbles in the vast cosmic landscape?

Think back to the moment you entered this world—a pure, innocent being carrying the universe's infinite potential within you. You weren't concerned with wealth, status, or success in that first cry of life. You simply *were*—whole, complete, and already worthy.

Every single one of us began our journey as perfect expressions of life itself. Observe any baby: they do not question their right to be nourished, loved, or cared for. They trust that their needs will be met. This isn't mere instinct—it embodies divine knowing, a remembrance of our true nature as beings of infinite worth and boundless potential.

As we grew older, society began to layer conditioning over our pure knowing. We learned to doubt our worthiness. We're taught that money must be struggled for, and we must prove ourselves deserving. These veils obscure the remembrance of our authentic, abundant nature.

But beneath these veils, the truth remains unchanged: abundance is your birthright. Just as a flower doesn't question its right to bloom, you need not ask for your right to thrive in all areas of your life.

Consider how nature operates: does a tree question whether it deserves to grow tall? Does a bird doubt its ability to fly? Does a river wonder if it's worthy to flow to the sea? Everything in nature exists in a natural abundance, following its divine design without hesitation.

You are part of this exact nature. Your existence itself is proof of your right to abundance. The same force that grows forests and moves planets flows through you, supporting your unique expression of life.

The path to elevating your self-worth begins with recognition—not just of your skills and talents but of your inherent value as conscious beings. This recognition must go deeper than intellectual understanding; it must penetrate to the cellular level of your being.

When you chose to incarnate into this physical form, you brought a sacred contract with a divine purpose and destiny uniquely your own. Like a seed containing the full potential of a mighty oak, you arrived complete with everything needed to fulfill your cosmic purpose.

Think of great masters and teachers throughout history. They didn't start as masters—they started as babies, just like you. Their greatness wasn't acquired; it was unveiled. Their abundance unraveled when they aligned themselves to their true divine purpose by valuing themselves wholly to live a life authentic to who they truly are, fully and wholly as their true cosmic self.

Your unique gifts—whether they're in art, business, healing, teaching, or any other field—are not random accidents. They are divine expressions seeking to manifest through you. When you deny your worth, you're not just limiting yourself; you're limiting the flow of divine expression through you into the world. It's about knowing that you have something unique to offer, that your presence is a contribution, and that receiving financial prosperity is a natural byproduct of your unique service.

Your purpose isn't something you need to create—it's already encoded in your very being. Just as an acorn contains the blueprint of an oak tree, you contain the blueprint of your highest destiny. Your talents, passions, and even your challenges are not random—they are breadcrumbs leading you toward your divine purpose.

When we truly value ourselves, the universe responds in kind. Opportunities that once seemed out of reach suddenly appear within grasp. This isn't magic—it's the natural law of resonance. When you vibrate at the frequency of confidence and self-worth, you naturally attract experiences that match this vibration.

Confidence is currency. People who believe in their value attract opportunities like a magnet. They ask for the raise, launch the business, take the risks—and the universe responds in kind. This isn't woo-woo nonsense; it's how energy works. When you *own* your worth, the world reflects it right back at you.

Think of yourself as a lighthouse. When you shine bright, the ships of opportunities, money, and success find their way to you. When you dim yourself down with doubt and self-sabotage, you stay invisible.

Your sense of self-worth isn't just a psychological state—it's an energetic frequency that ripples through the quantum field, attracting or repelling abundance according to its vibration. When you feel worthy, you allow yourself to open to receive with open hands.

When you truly value yourself, you radiate confidence that resonates with abundance. When you are confident, you hold 100% certainty and believe in yourself with zero resistance. When you have low self-worth, you emit self-doubt energies where people will question you suspiciously. The world responds to how you see yourself.

True confidence flourishes when we choose to love and respect ourselves unconditionally. To gain confidence and self-worth, love yourself first. Build your self-esteem by doing actions and being the person who makes you proud of who you are.

True abundance flows not from what you do but from who you are.

You become a natural conduit for abundance when you align with your authentic self-worth. Your unique combination of talents, experiences, and insights is unrepeatable in the universe's history. This uniqueness isn't just your gift—it's your responsibility to share your wisdom with the world.

Imagine you are a little seed, and all the fertilizer is life experiences that are forming you, with the richness of life experiences preparing your hero's journey on the verge of something epic. Inside that tiny shell is a force so powerful that it has the potential to burst through the soil, stretch toward the sky, and transform into a mighty oak or a radiant sunflower.

You're that seed. And life? Life is the soil pressing in on you from every angle, daring you to grow. Challenges, setbacks, failures, and heartbreaks aren't roadblocks; they're the very things that sculpt you into the goddess you're meant to become.

That shell? It's not going to crack open just because the seed politely asks. Unlike a seed, you have willpower, choices, and free will to transform your life experiences into wisdom. To sprout, the seed has to push. It has to struggle. It has to face the hardships of life—it's the training ground. As the seed, you have to extract every vitamin and mineral of life lessons to break free and through. You have to push through resistance that will come in the form of comfort, distraction, & escape. Every ounce of pressure isn't there to stop you; it's there to ensure that when you finally emerge, you're strong enough to stand tall.

Every wildly successful person—every artist, athlete, entrepreneur, and game-changer—has faced gut-wrenching hardships. They've been rejected, doubted, ridiculed, and knocked flat on their backs. But instead of seeing hardships as personal failures that weren't good enough, they extracted the lessons they needed to learn from them. They didn't quit. They pushed harder. They broke through. And so can you.

A tree that grows in perfect conditions—no wind, no storms, no obstacles—ends up weak. Its roots are shallow, its trunk is flimsy, and it snaps like a twig at the first sign of trouble. But a tree that battles the elements? That one sends its roots deep, stands firm, and weathers every storm like a champ.

You are not here to be fragile. You are here to express your greatness. And that only happens when you embrace the struggle and use it to build the resilience that turns ordinary people into legends.

Growth isn't comfortable. Becoming your next-level self will feel like stretching muscles you didn't even know you had. It will require breaking through old habits, confronting your fears, and stepping into uncertainty with nothing but faith and determination.

So the next time you feel overwhelmed, ask yourself: Am I being buried or planted? The truth is, it's all in how you respond. You can either let resistance keep you down or rise.

Don't get stuck in the dirt with the comfort of being unseen—breakthrough through to the other side, where a whole new life blooms. Rise to your innate power and greatness.

This is the secret to financial success: It is not about chasing money but about becoming the version of yourself who naturally receives it. When you embody your worth, abundance no longer remains a distant pursuit—it becomes an inevitable reality.

You do not need to wait for external validation to affirm your value. The moment you truly decide that you are worthy, the universe begins to rearrange itself in response. Opportunities emerge, synchronicities unfold, and the doors that once seemed closed begin to open effortlessly.

The journey to financial prosperity begins with the sacred act of recognizing your inherent worth. Like an alchemist transforming lead into gold, you must transform these limiting beliefs into golden truths about your value. As you elevate your self-worth, you elevate your entire existence, creating ripples of possibility that extend far beyond your individual life.

Abundance is not a zero-sum game. Your wealth does not diminish the wealth of others; rather, it expands the collective flow. When you allow yourself to receive fully, you create a ripple effect beyond you. Your prosperity inspires others to step into their own worth. Your financial freedom enables you to contribute, give, and uplift those around you.

In the divine economy of the universe, the more you receive, the more you can give—and the more you give, the more space you create for receiving. This continuous, expansive cycle begins with a single individual making a huge impact.

Remember: You are not here to play small. You are here to shine in your full brilliance, to receive abundantly, and to let your prosperity be a light that illuminates the path for others. The time for dimming your light is over. The time to embrace your worth is now.

7

Your Emotions & Your Money

Let's venture into the wild jungle of our spending habits, untangling the tempestuous snake of emotional psychology wriggling through our wallet decisions. Get ready to illuminate those shadowy corners where your emotions secretly pull the spending strings. This journey will unlock revelations that reveal your emotional and fiscal connection.

Your emotions are not just fluttery feelings but influence and stealthily call the shots in your daily expenditures. Neuroscientist Antonio Damasio, with a mind-blowing theory called the somatic marker hypothesis, informs us that our emotions don't just influence but steer our behaviors and decisions. These emotional markers bubble up from our bodily sensations, slide into our cognitive processes, and silently influence our choices, which can sometimes override our logical reasoning.

Shockingly, even the brainiacs blessed with logical superpowers, if stripped of emotions, find themselves wading through the vast, confusing sea of overwhelming decision-making. Without emotional anchors, their logically sound choices become a dicey journey through a swamp of indecision and complexity. Emotions are a large part of our decisions, elegantly linking our past memories with present ones. They are our personal inner guide for each choice we make.

Imagine navigating life's perplexing choices without these purposeful emotional nudges—every decision balloons into a mountainous challenge for those who are cognitive wizards but emotional zombies. Every choice morphs into an eternal battle against an avalanche of baffling options without personal preferences that make up who we individually are.

Our emotions are far more than transient feelings; they are the offscreen architects of subtly shaping our path, infusing our decisions with the resonances from our past. It's time to cast a shimmering spotlight on these emotions, acknowledging them as the invisible navigators directing our vessels through the turbulent seas of life's ceaseless choices. Bereft of emotional guidance, our logical faculties resemble ships adrift, aimless in an infinite sea.

These emotions are our internal compass in the vast, untamed wilderness of different options everywhere we go. Our personal emotions guide us, not arbitrarily, but in harmony with our deepest, intuitive selves. They chart our course, intertwining the threads of past connections with the fabric of our present lives. Emotions are not mere responses to external stimuli; they are integrally linked to our personal narratives, imbuing every decision with significance and subtly steering the course of our destiny.

Our emotions are personalized navigators, whispering directions for our choices, all based on our emotional history. Be it the hot coffee that nudges a cozy memory, the career path that sets our soul on fire, or the investment that stirs a flutter of anxiety - they're all choreographed by somatic markers, often whispering beneath our conscious radar. Beneath the calculated logic lurks an emotional guidance GPS, each wave a relic of past experiences, subtly guiding our present choices. These emotional currents can sway our financial decisions, and it's time to recognize and understand which emotional waves are steering us toward fiscal paradise or peril.

Emotional Spending

Have you ever felt a momentary rush of euphoria after a whimsy purchase that turned out wasn't something you necessarily needed? Or have you found yourself on a shopping spree, trying to buy your way out of feeling stressed, sad, or just plain bored? This is the emotional roller coaster ride of emotional spending! Emotions play a pivotal role in influencing our financial spending, often leading us down paths we never intended to tread.

At the core of emotional spending lies the psychological triggers that prompt us to reach for our wallets with compulsion. Let's explore some of the most common ones:

Retail Therapy: Emotional spending is often linked to the concept of "retail therapy," where shopping becomes a coping mechanism for stress or emotional distress. The temporary high we experience when making a purchase can act as a distraction from life's challenges, but it's essential to recognize this response and find healthier ways to deal with our emotions.

Identity and Self-Worth: Our purchases can be an extension of our identity and self-worth. Buying specific brands or items may make us feel more confident or accepted within our social circles. Understanding this aspect of spending helps us question whether we're buying for ourselves or to impress others.

Instant Gratification: In today's fast-paced world, we crave instant gratification. Purchasing something new provides immediate pleasure, which can lead us to prioritize short-term happiness over long-term financial well-being. That quick fix, that one-click "Buy Now" button, satiates our cravings instantly. Next time, pause and ask yourself if that instant gratification is worth the long-term financial hangover of sometimes even overpaying with high interest rates.

Fear of Missing Out (FOMO): Social media and advertising capitalize on our fear of missing out on the latest trends or exclusive deals. This fear can push us to make impulsive purchases, even when we don't truly need the item or experience.

Master Your Emotions

Fear often dictates our financial behaviors—fear of losing money, fear of making the wrong choice, fear of never having enough. The goal isn't to eliminate fear but to learn to coexist with it without letting it dictate your decisions.

When market downturns trigger anxiety, remind yourself that volatility is temporary, but wise investments endure. When the weight of debt feels crushing, focus on incremental progress rather than the enormity of the total amount. Acknowledge financial fear, but do not allow it to control your days.

Money decisions happen amid the emotional currents of daily life—stress from work, celebration of milestones, or moments of self-doubt. You're stressed from work? Boom—impulse buy. Celebrating a win? Hello, fancy dinner. Feeling stuck? Swipe, add to cart, repeat. Financial presence is the ability to maintain awareness of your spending habits and investment choices, even in emotionally charged situations.

The next time you feel the urge to spend, pause. Tune in. Are you excited? Anxious? Trying to self-soothe? These gut reactions are physical signals that often reveal deep-seated money triggers. But guess what? You're in the pilot's seat. Recognizing these emotional money triggers gives you the power to break the cycle and choose **wisely** instead of reactively. By recognizing them, you create a crucial moment of separation between impulse and action—a space where financial wisdom can take root.

Rituals for Emotional Mastery

Each day presents a series of financial crossroads. The seemingly minor decisions—whether to grab a coffee on the way to work, browse an online sale, or choose a lunch option—quickly add up over time, subtly sculpting our financial realities. These micro-decisions, often made on autopilot, either build or erode our financial stability.

To anchor yourself in financial consciousness, begin your day by taking one powerful minute for yourself—your Morning Money Minute. Before checking emails or diving into the day's obligations, take sixty seconds to reflect on your financial intentions. Picture your savings stacking up like bricks in your financial fortress. Imagine the freedom that comes from being in control of your money instead of letting it control you. This ritual sets the tone for deliberate and aligned financial choices throughout the day. This is a powerful intention-setting exercise that keeps you aligned with your financial goals before the world starts pulling you in a million directions.

Consider reframing financial tasks as acts of empowerment rather than burdens.

- **Paying bills with gratitude**: Instead of dreading bill payments, see them as affirmations of your ability to provide for yourself and your loved ones.
- **Saving with purpose**: View each contribution to your savings or investment accounts as a step toward future security and freedom, not merely an obligation.
- **Tracking spending with curiosity**: Instead of judging past financial choices, approach them with curiosity. What patterns emerge? What emotions drive your spending?

By transforming routine money tasks into meaningful rituals, financial habits become second nature rather than sources of resistance.

The Emotional Wealth Indicator

True financial success isn't solely measured by net worth but by the quality of your relationship with money. Ask yourself:

- Do I feel anxious or empowered when making financial decisions?
- Can I delay gratification for long-term gains?
- Do I approach money with confidence rather than avoidance?

These questions reveal your emotional wealth—an invaluable asset that directly impacts financial outcomes. A healthy financial mindset leads to better decision-making and an overall sense of control and fulfillment.

The Journey of Financial Mastery

Financial growth is not a straight path; it is an ongoing journey marked by learning, setbacks, and progress. There will be days when old habits resurface, when emotions override logic, or when financial goals feel distant. The key is not perfection but resilience—the ability to return, time and again, to the practice of emotional mastery & money management.

Through daily financial presence & intentional rituals you transform money from emotional chaos into mastery for building the life you desire. Your emotional relationship with money determines your financial future so work on it like your future depends on it—because it does.

Be Conscientious

Consider adopting a strategy known as *conscientious spending*, a vital aspect of personal finance that can lead you to financial freedom and stability. Conscientious spending is the art of making deliberate, mindful, and informed decisions about where you allocate your hard-earned money. By incorporating conscientious spending habits into your daily life, you can create a budget that is effective and more likely to be sustainable over the long term. It's time to create a budget that aligns with your goals and values.

Conscientious spending goes beyond mere budgeting; it involves developing a mindful and intentional approach to your financial choices. It starts with cultivating awareness of your spending patterns and understanding the deeper reasons behind your purchases. By recognizing your values and priorities, you can ensure that your spending aligns with your long-term goals, whether they be saving for a dream vacation, building an emergency fund, or investing for your future. You're not just some mindless money-spender; you're a savvy, conscious spender who knows exactly where every dollar goes and why! Get ready to be the boss of your spending rather than succumbing to the whims of momentary emotions.

Through introspection, you'll recognize that your values are not generic but unique markers that define you. For some, family might be paramount, while others might prioritize personal growth, social impact, or adventure. Acknowledging these values will empower you to align your financial decisions accordingly. From impactful investors who support businesses making a difference to philanthropists who use their wealth to improve the world, it demonstrates how money, when aligned with values, can leave a lasting legacy. Intention becomes the focal point when we emphasize the importance of being purposeful with every monetary action. When you connect your financial endeavors with your core values, your money transforms from mere currency into a ripple effect of forces for positive change. Your finances metamorphose from simple monetary units to catalysts of benevolent change, sending ripples of positivity through the fabric of society.

Even after recognizing the connection between values and money, you may face challenges in realigning your financial decisions. One major obstacle is societal pressure and materialistic culture advertised to you every way you turn, which often push us away from our true values. These external forces, with their siren calls of instant gratification, frequently steer us astray from our authentic selves. This is why it's essential to be grounded in your values and to know what truly matters deeply most to you. It's time to identify and get clear on your values. What matters most to you right now? What do you want for your future?

1. **Self-Reflection:** Take some time to reflect on what matters most to you in life. Consider your long-term goals, aspirations, and what brings you true fulfillment and happiness. Think about the

areas of your life that you value the most, such as family, health, personal growth, career, hobbies, travel, charity, etc.

2. **Make a List:** Write down your values and priorities. Be specific about what each value means to you and how it contributes to your overall well-being and happiness.

3. **Rank Your Values:** Prioritize your values based on their significance to you. This will help you allocate your finances more effectively in alignment with what matters most.

4. **Assess Current Spending:** Review your past spending habits and analyze where your money has been going. Compare your spending with the values you've listed. Are you currently spending in a way that aligns with your values, or are there areas where your spending doesn't reflect your priorities?

5. **Set Clear Financial Goals:** Based on your values and priorities, establish specific financial goals for each area of importance. For example, if health and fitness are important, you might set a goal to allocate a certain amount of money each month for a gym membership or healthy food options.

6. **Create a Budget:** Use your values and financial goals as a foundation for creating a budget plan. Allocate your income to the various categories, ensuring that you are giving more weight to the areas that align with your top values.

7. **Cut Unnecessary Expenses:** Identify any expenses that don't align with your values and consider cutting them or reducing their allocation. This might include subscriptions, take-out, or other non-essential spending.

8. **Track and Adjust:** As you start following your budget plan, track your spending regularly. This will help you stay accountable and make adjustments if needed. Life circumstances and priorities can change, so be open to modifying your budget as necessary.

9. **Practice Discipline and Flexibility:** Sticking to a budget requires

discipline, especially when it comes to aligning your spending with your values. However, be flexible enough to accommodate unexpected expenses or changes in your priorities.

10. **Building Resilience:** Strengthen your emotional resilience to cope with stress and negative emotions without resorting to retail therapy. Engage in activities that promote well-being, such as exercise, hobbies, or spending quality time with loved ones.

11. **Practicing Delayed Gratification:** Challenge yourself to practice delayed gratification. If you're tempted to make an impulse purchase, wait for a few days and evaluate whether it's still something you truly want or need.

12. **Celebrate Progress:** As you make progress towards your financial goals and witness how your budget plan enables you to support your values, take the time to celebrate your achievements. This positive reinforcement can motivate you to continue living within the means that align with your values.

One of the fundamental pillars of conscientious spending is meticulous planning. To create a budget that works for you, you must be willing to invest time and effort in assessing your financial situation comprehensively. Begin by calculating your total income and identifying all your essential expenses, such as rent or mortgage, utilities, groceries, and debt payments. With a clear understanding of your fixed expenses, you can make informed decisions about your discretionary spending. Knowledge is power, and once you know where your money's going, you can reclaim control like a true money boss!

Next, divide your discretionary spending into categories based on their significance and alignment with your values. For example, create categories aligned to your values like "health," "wishlist," and "savings/investments." Health should include expenses that directly contribute to your priorities at the moment, such as fitness classes, organic foods, and non-toxic household items. Wishlists encompass expenses that provide enjoyment or leisure but may not be crucial to your overall well-being. Savings and investments are critical for securing your financial future and should be given priority.

With your expenses categorized, set clear and realistic financial goals for each category. Define specific targets for saving, investing, and discretionary spending. Remember that your goals should be challenging yet attainable, motivating you to stay on track without becoming overwhelmed. Prioritize your goals based on their importance, ensuring that essential objectives are funded before allocating money to less critical ones.

Now that you have a clear understanding of your financial situation and goals, it's time to create your budget. Utilize spreadsheets, budgeting apps, or good old pen and paper – whatever suits you best. Create a monthly budget, taking into account your income, fixed expenses, and discretionary spending categories. Allocate funds to each category based on your financial goals, and remember to leave some room for unforeseen expenses or occasional treats.

To enhance your conscientious spending journey, consider implementing the envelope system for certain discretionary spending categories. Set aside cash in designated envelopes for activities like dining out, entertainment, or shopping. This method prevents overspending by providing a tangible limit and encourages you to be more mindful of your choices. Most often there is a bit more resistance in spending concrete visible cash versus the swift tap of a 2-second credit card transaction.

A budget requires ongoing monitoring and adjustments. Regularly review your spending habits to ensure you're staying on track with your financial goals. Check your bank account every day. Analyze your progress, celebrate your achievements, and learn from any mistakes and oversights. Be flexible and willing to make changes to your budget as your circumstances evolve.

Conscientious spending is a mindful method that can help you gain control over your finances and build financial well-being. By incorporating meticulous planning and creating a budget that aligns with your values and aspirations, you can make sensible spending decisions and achieve your financial goals. Remember, it's not just about constantly restricting yourself from spending; it's about making intentional choices that lead to fulfilling financial decisions that you won't regret. Take charge of your financial well-being, and embark on the path to ultimate financial health with conscientious spending as your new habit.

Congratulations! By now, you've learned how to budget with conscientious spending. You've discovered the power of creating a budget, setting financial goals, and making informed and mindful decisions about your money. Now, it's time to elevate your financial journey to enjoy budgeting and finances, transforming it from a mundane task to a fulfilling and empowering part of your life. Finances don't have to be a dread; you can make your finances fun! Your mindset and attitude set the tone for how you feel about money. Create a positive money attitude by loving your budget and creating a "treat yourself" or "self-care" category.

Budgeting is often perceived as restricting, but it's crucial to understand that it offers unparalleled freedom. A positive mindset shift is the first step toward making budgeting enjoyable. Budgeting is not about depriving yourself, no way! It's about taking charge of your cash flow and planning for the life you've always dreamed of! Think of your budget as a map, guiding you toward your financial goals and dreams. Imagine the rewards or where you'll be in 1 year or 5 years if you stick to your budget plan. The key along your journey is *delayed gratification*!

Create a reward system if you follow your budget every month, and you can reward yourself with some sort of prize! You need to set aside a budget for joy for yourself to experience enjoying money. Set mini-goals within your budget and celebrate them. Whether it's paying off a credit card, funding an emergency fund, or successfully sticking to your budget for a month, acknowledge your progress with small rewards that won't break the bank. Reward yourself for each milestone, whether it's treating yourself to a fancy coffee or a day off at the beach. Celebrate your wins along the way, no matter how small. It's all about progress!

Start each budgeting session by reminding yourself of your grand financial aspirations. Visualize the life you want to lead and how financial discipline will help you get there. Embrace the journey, knowing that each dollar you allocate is a step closer to living the life of your dreams.

Create a ritual around budgeting whether be it daily, weekly, or monthly. Before diving into those numbers, light your favorite scented candle and meditate for 5-10 minutes invoking positive energy towards budgeting. Play your favorite song and repeat affirmations like "I'm a money queen" or "I'm the boss of my finances!" And after each budgeting session, you can do a little happy dance or cheer, be your biggest cheerleader!

Budgeting doesn't have to be a rigid and boring exercise. It can be a creative outlet where you get to design the life you desire. Everyone's budget is different and unique according to their personal lifestyle. Someone will budget for a sailboat, and someone else will budget for hiking Mt.Everest. By embracing creativity in budgeting, you'll find joy in exploring different ways to allocate your resources effectively. Create themed budget categories that reflect your values and passions. For instance, allocate a portion of your budget to "Hobbies" or "Vacations." This way, budgeting becomes an enjoyable process to experience how money can be allocated to bring you gratification and happiness.

Achieving financial goals is a journey that requires dedication and persistence. Celebrate each milestone along the way to keep the momentum going. Acknowledge the small successes as they pave the way for more significant achievements. Let's give those small wins the high-fives they deserve 'cause they're the stepping stones to your big, bold financial victories. Even if you paid off a tiny debt or saved a few bucks, you're making waves!

Finances don't have to be a solitary experience. Meet with others who share your financial goals and aspirations for accountability. Join communities, attend workshops, or seek financial accountability partners to share your journey. Surround yourself with like-minded individuals who uplift and inspire you on your financial journey. You can discuss financial goals and celebrate each other's achievements by throwing large celebration parties. Share budgeting tips, swap money-saving hacks, and support each other in reaching those financial dreams. Together, you'll create a tribe of money-smart squads changing each other's lives, one budget at a time!

Turn your budgeting process into a game with challenges, achievements, and rewards with a technique known as *gamification*. Gamification can make even the most mundane tasks enjoyable by turning an activity into a fun game. You can download those fun budgeting apps and turn budgeting into a thrilling game. Set challenges for yourself, and remember you make the rules! Compete with yourself, beat your best scores, and give yourself a high-five in the mirror when you crush those goals. You're not just budgeting; you're leveling up your life! Bring your enthusiastic spirit to make budgeting fun and a rewarding experience to bring joy to your budgeting routine!

Remember that your budget is a tool for achieving your dreams and aligning your money with your values. Embrace the process, celebrate your progress, and keep a positive mindful money attitude. As you continue to infuse joy into budgeting, you'll not only master your finances but you'll also lead a fulfilling and abundant life.

8

Self-Identity

reating deep change does not happen overnight; for real, lasting change, it requires the development of new habits, thoughts, and behaviors that rewire our brains to create a new version of ourselves. At first, it's natural to feel like a stranger in the realm of wealth. You might feel unfamiliar with being rich and, therefore, feel uncomfortable with it. You may not identify as a millionaire magically in the blink of an eye. Still, you can incrementally grow to feel comfortable making an extra $1,000 until it becomes a million. It is paramount that you cultivate an unshakable sense of comfort and security in the presence of greater wealth entering your life. You must cultivate a feeling of safety with more money as you grow your wealth so you don't blindly self-sabotage it by manifesting sudden and voracious expenses. This starts with the inner work of building your identity as a wealthy person and imagining what kind of person you dream of being as your ideal wealthy self. And as you nurture these inner seeds of your new identity, watering them with consistency and belief, you'll find yourself draped in the riches of life's offerings.

Imagine sitting on a plush, velvety couch in your luxurious penthouse, the skyline of your favorite city twinkling outside your floor-to-ceiling windows. You've just closed a deal that's added an extra zero or two to your bank account, and now, you're sipping a glass of something bubbly, feeling on top of the world. This, my friend, is your future wealthy self, or just imagine your own version. But to make this vision a reality, you must start embodying that wealthy you *today.*

While most seek financial transformation through knowledge alone—reading books, attending seminars, consuming endless content—the deeper truth remains: wealth is not something you know but something you become. This becoming happens by embodying the wealthy version of you now in every aspect of your being through your thoughts, energy, actions, and the thousand tiny choices that compose each day.

Through embodiment, your energy tells the Universe you are in abundance, and it will respond accordingly. Wealth creation follows the same principle. True financial manifestation emerges not from theoretical understanding but from "acting as if" in the now.

To manifest wealth, you have to first believe you are already abundant. Then, you have to act in accordance with the belief that you are abundant. You have to embody the identity of a wealthy person. Create your self-identity as a wealthy person. Who is this wealthy version of you? And how would they behave? What choices would they make? Write in detail describing this wealthy version of yourself on a Post-it and put it in your mirror or somewhere you can see daily to remind yourself to be that person now. The fastest way to becoming this wealthy version of yourself is to be that person now! Every day in your current reality, embody this wealthy version of yourself by making decisions that align with your wealthiest version. Be that person now by thinking what they would think, feeling how they would feel, and behaving as that wealthiest version of you in every situation. Would they be thinking positive thoughts? What would abundance feel like on a daily basis? What decisions would you make today if you were the wealthiest version of yourself now? What can you do today to be closer to the wealthiest version of yourself?

Now, it's time to bring this vision into your present reality. Start by making choices that align with your wealthy identity. It could be as simple as the way you dress, the conversations you engage in, or the routines you establish. If your wealthy self is fit and energetic, hit the gym. If they are knowledgeable and savvy, start learning something new every day. Even if it's just a small step, keep going! Most importantly, do things to feel abundant; the feeling is the secret! Remember, with gratitude, even the small things in life can feel phenomenally abundant, such as your health or even your breath!

Journal Magic

Start by praying to your angels and guides to channel writing through you with gratitude. Ask your future wealthiest version of yourself for guidance, asking any burning question of your heart's desire. Continue writing for three pages nonstop, even if you get off topic.

After your writing session, what insights, answers, or guidance revealed themselves? Highlight them!

Becoming

Every financial choice is a movement that either aligns with or deviates from your wealthy identity. The coffee you buy, the subscription you renew, the investment you consider—each represents a moment of choreography in your wealth creation. The question isn't "What should I do?" but "Who am I becoming through this choice?"

Wealthy individuals don't simply think differently about money— they move through the world differently. Their posture, energy, and presence all reflect a deep alignment with abundance. This alignment wasn't achieved just by wishing but through intention and choices that gradually rewired not just their minds but their entire way of being.

To be wealthy, you must feel wealthy first. If you are feeling fearful or anxious about money, you are energetically repelling money. You have to start allowing your body to learn new ways of being with money. Take small steps to start feeling at ease with money—and lots of it! Let your shoulders drop when reviewing your finances. Let your breath deepen when paying your bills. Let your voice find its natural authority when discussing money.

When you first step into greater wealth, the sensation may feel foreign, even uncomfortable—like wearing a suit that doesn't quite fit. This discomfort isn't a sign of unworthiness but of growth. You may get excited about a new check of $10,000 coming your way, but you may also feel uncomfortable about it if you've never had that much money before. Just as a muscle feels tender when stretched in new ways, your financial identity may feel stretched as it expands to embrace abundance. Wealth consciousness develops in much the same way— through gradual exposure, openness, and growing trust in your capacity to navigate larger numbers.

The path to wealth isn't about leaping from hundreds to millions overnight. It's about expanding your comfort zone dollar by dollar, decision by decision. Begin where you are. If handling an extra thousand dollars feels uncomfortable, start there. Let yourself fully experience what it feels like to earn, save, and manage that amount with confidence.

As you master each level, your capacity naturally expands. The thousand that once felt overwhelming becomes comfortable. The ten thousand that seemed impossible becomes achievable. Like rings in a tree, your wealth consciousness grows through steady accumulation, each layer building upon the last.

Just as a gardener creates optimal conditions for growth, you must create internal conditions that welcome and sustain wealth. This starts with cultivating a sense of safety around money. Your nervous system needs to know that greater wealth won't threaten your equilibrium.

Begin by creating small moments of financial peace. Light a candle when reviewing your accounts. Play soft music while paying bills. Create rituals that help your body associate money management with calm and centeredness rather than stress and anxiety.

Consider the difference between knowing you should save and feeling like a person who saves naturally. The first is intellectual; the second is embodied. The bridge between these states is built through repeatedly choosing behaviors that align with your desired identity until they become as natural as breathing. Every time you embody wealth by feeling abundance, you are magnetizing abundance to you. As you make every decision as your wealthiest version of yourself in your current reality, you will come to grow into fit in that once oversized million-dollar suit.

True financial transformation happens when your actions, thoughts, and identity align into a seamless whole. This alignment isn't achieved through force but through embodying the identity of the wealthy you —through showing up day after day, choice after choice, gradually allowing your wealthy identity to emerge through consistent action.

In the pursuit of wealth, we often focus on what we'll have while overlooking who we'll be. Yet the most profound question isn't about the size of your bank account—it's about the depth of your character. Your wealthy identity isn't something you'll discover once you've achieved financial success; it's something you're crafting right now in every decision, every interaction, and every moment of choice.

Your future wealth is being shaped not by market conditions or investment strategies but by the character you're developing today. When you imagine your wealthy self, look beyond the material trappings. What values will guide your decisions? How will you treat others? What legacy will you create? These questions matter more than any financial projection.

Our wealthy identity lies in who we are becoming. What kind of wealthy person will you be? Develop your character now as that wealthy person. The choices you make and the actions you take reflect who you are. So, who do you want to be?

Consider the wealthy person you aspire to be. Are they generous or guarded? Humble or ostentatious? Do they use their resources to lift others or to separate themselves? The answers reveal not just your financial aspirations but your deeper values—the foundation upon which lasting wealth is built.

You need not wait for wealth to embody these qualities. If you envision yourself as a philanthropic millionaire, start practicing generosity now, even with limited resources. If you see yourself as a wise investor, begin cultivating discernment in your daily choices. If you imagine being a mentor to others, start sharing your knowledge and support today.

Each moment offers an opportunity to align your actions with your wealthy character. When facing decisions, ask, "What would the wealthy person I aspire to do?" This subtle shift transforms routine choices into character-building moments.

True wealth flows most naturally to those whose character can sustain it. Like a house built on solid foundations, wealth built on strong character weathers the storms of circumstance. This foundation is laid brick by brick through countless small acts of integrity.

Paying bills promptly even when funds are tight. Honoring commitments even when more lucrative opportunities arise. Speaking truth even when silence would be more profitable. These moments shape not just your reputation but your capacity to create and grow wealth.

Character isn't formed in grand moments but in quiet choices when no one is watching: the decision to save rather than spend, the choice to invest in learning rather than indulging in distraction, and the commitment to long-term growth over short-term gratification.

Your wealthy identity emerges from these choices. Each time you choose in alignment with your highest values, you strengthen the character that will attract and sustain wealth. Each time you compromise those values, you weaken the foundation of your future house of prosperity.

How you treat others on your path to wealth reveals and shapes your character. Do you view relationships as transactions or opportunities for mutual growth? Do you seek to dominate or collaborate? Do you share your knowledge or hoard it?

The wealthy character you're developing will be reflected in every interaction. Practice being the person you aspire to be in all your relationships—with family, colleagues, employees, and strangers. Let your interactions be guided by the values you want your wealth to express.

True wealth brings not just abundance but responsibility. Begin developing a stewardship mindset now. See yourself not as the owner of resources but as their custodian, responsible for their wise use and multiplication.

This perspective transforms how you handle even modest resources. Every dollar becomes an opportunity to practice wise stewardship, every possession becomes a chance to demonstrate care and responsibility, and every investment becomes an expression of your values.

The character of true wealth is also marked by generosity. This isn't about grand philanthropic gestures but about cultivating a giving spirit in all areas of life. Be generous with your time, your knowledge, your encouragement, your resources—whatever you have to share.

You can start where you are. Find ways to contribute that align with your values and vision. Let your giving be an expression of who you're becoming, not just what you have. This practice of generosity expands your capacity to receive.

Consider not just what you want to achieve but what you want to leave behind. Your wealthy character will create ripples that extend far beyond your immediate circle. What impact do you want your wealth to have? What values do you want to transmit? What example do you want to set?

As your wealthy character develops, you'll find that who you are becoming naturally attracts what you seek to have. The qualities you cultivate—integrity, wisdom, generosity, and responsibility—create an energetic field that supports lasting prosperity.

Wealth without character is like a house built on sand. But character aligned with wealth creates a foundation for lasting impact. Focus first on becoming the person worthy of the wealth you seek, and the path to that wealth will become clear.

Your wealthy character isn't a destination but a continuous evolution. Each new level of success will present fresh opportunities for growth, new challenges to your values, and deeper calls to wisdom and integrity. Embrace this ongoing development. Let each experience refine your character. In the end, the greatest wealth you'll possess isn't what's in your bank account but who you've become in the process of creating it.

Rather than waiting to feel wealthy, understand that the feeling magnetizes results. Each time you choose in alignment with your wealthy identity, you strengthen the neural pathways that make such choices to embody wealth and attract it into your life.

This path requires faith—the faith to act differently before seeing results, the courage to birth a new identity to emerge through embodying abundance now. Manifesting a wealthy identity is about quiet persistence, about showing up repeatedly through the practice of becoming.

Your wealthy identity already exists within you. You are the gold covered in layers of fear and doubt that make the mud cover your greatness. The journey isn't about trying to be someone else but about removing the blocks—physical, emotional, and energetic—that prevent your authentic identity from fully expressing itself.

The embodied path to wealth never ends, for there is always deeper alignment to embody, greater wisdom to discover, and more profound ways to experience wealth consciousness. Each day brings new opportunities to practice and new chances to align your physical reality with your expansion. The Universe is limitless, and so is your expansion.

Welcome these opportunities not as challenges to overcome but as invitations to embody your wealth more fully, more authentically, to the highest limits you can reach. For in this embodiment lies the true secret of lasting financial transformation—not in what you know, but in who you become through consistent, aligned action.

Surround Yourself with Inspiration

You are the average of the five people you spend the most time with. So, choose wisely. Surround yourself with individuals who inspire you and challenge you to level up with support. If your current circle is more about comfort zones and less about growth, it's time to make some changes.

Join groups or communities where high achievers hang out. Attend events where you can meet people who are already living the life you aspire to. Their energy, insights, and attitudes will naturally expand you, propelling you further on your journey to abundance.

The Universe is Listening

By acting as if you're already wealthy, you're sending a powerful message to the universe: "I am abundance." This isn't just about wishful thinking; it's about aligning your actions with your desires. The universe responds to the energy you put out, and when you operate from a place of abundance and confidence, it mirrors that back to you.

So, start today. Make that bold decision. Face that challenge with moxie. Spend your time wisely. Invest in yourself. Surround yourself with greatness. Take that risk. Every action you take from this point forward should be a reflection of the wealthy you. Aim to be the best version of yourself and expect greatness from within because, like nature intended lions to be majestic, you are capable of achieving extraordinary things alike. With the support of riches behind you to support you, you can do greater and grander things to expand humanity. Most importantly, you can express your soul's essence as it was meant to. Be the rich you now by embodying the characteristics of the future you, even if you have to start in little ways like dressing the part, acting the part, and being the part today. It all starts in the mind to think about the part first and then actively create it. Be it today, to be the money magnet tomorrow.

9

Money is Neutral

Despite money's ubiquitous presence, we find ourselves stumbling around the subject, often unable to talk about it without a sense of unease or discomfort. First, it is essential to recognize that influence traces back from our parents, grandparents, and so on over generations. We've been warned since we were knee-high that "talking about money is impolite," and we've taken it as gospel. Such sentiments echoed in households and communities over generations have ingrained a kind of monetary taboo in our collective psyche. But actually, when you don't communicate, it just causes more confusion for everyone.

Money, for better or worse, is a universally recognized yardstick of success. One major reason we zip our lips when it comes to money is that nobody likes to be judged. Discussing finances, therefore, opens the door to judgment based on our income, savings, or spending. We live in a world where money equals success, and showing your financial cards means opening yourself up to scrutiny. Are you a big spender? A penny-pincher? Caught in a perpetual loop of being broke? Welcome to the Judgment Olympics. The fear of being perceived as too poor, too lavish, or too miserly often silences us before the conversation can even

96

start.

Another aspect contributing to our unease around money is its intimate relationship with our values and self-esteem. Money can act as a mirror, reflecting our priorities, choices, and compromises. We buy what we value. We save and spend based on what we deem important. To discuss money is to lay bare these personal choices and values for others to critique. It's no wonder that we often prefer to keep these discussions off the table. Our money choices are like our own personal reality show, and who wants to air that season premiere?

Our lack of financial knowledge stems from a lack of financial literacy. The discomfort around money talk often acts as a barrier to the acquisition of crucial financial skills. This is a vicious cycle - we don't talk about money because we're uncomfortable, and we're uncomfortable because we lack knowledge about it.

This lack of financial knowledge stems from grade school. We are taught every subject except the most basic and essential life skill of personal finances. This makes the topic of money even more taboo because maybe if we studied it, we wouldn't be as unstably emotional about it. Imagine you, fresh out of school, armed with a deep understanding of the Pythagorean theorem, the symbolism in *Romeo and Juliet*, and the exact process of photosynthesis. Yet, the moment a credit card offer lands in your mailbox, you are frivolously spending what seems to be some sort of magical plastic card because —no one ever taught you what the hell a credit card is or how interest fees work.

If your family didn't teach you about money, surprise —you've been winging it. So, instead, you're living life with a hand-me-down money style from your old folks. Whether we realize it or not, we tend to copy what we saw growing up. If your parents lived paycheck to paycheck, odds are, you learned that was normal. If money was a constant source of stress, you may have absorbed the belief that money is the root of all problems. It's like you're dropped into the middle of a jungle, blindfolded, with nothing but a plastic spoon and the vague memory of a survival show you watched once. That's basically how most of us enter adulthood when it comes to money.

School totally ghosted us on this topic, leaving us to stumble through our finances like a newborn giraffe—wobbly, clueless, and one bad decision away from face-planting into a pile of overdue bills. We're taught how to dissect a frog but not how to understand our credit card bills. We can rattle off historical dates like a trivia champ but have zero clue how to file taxes, build credit, or invest in our future. This is a systemic disaster that's setting people up for financial struggle, and then they end up being too behind to even start gaining any knowledge as they barely survive paycheck to paycheck. Many people are drowning in credit card debt, living paycheck to paycheck, and panicking about retirement because they were never taught the basics of personal finance. Stress over finances is one of the top causes of anxiety, fights in relationships, and sleepless nights. We were all thrown into a financial system that we were never trained to navigate from the beginning unless we had guidance from our parents or mentors, etc. Schools educate us to memorize the atomic number of carbon, and while a small population may become chemists, we can all benefit from a critical lesson on how to budget. We had to memorize the dates of historical wars in detail but were sent into adulthood, financially malnourished. I'm not saying we need to omit anything and that one subject is more important than another. I'm saying we need both, and why not learn about finances just as much as we're studying another language, which was a requirement in my high school? Every subject is valuable, but as we are learning meticulously about the periodic table and rehearsing Shakespeare, why not teach at least the basics of personal finances to teenagers who probably receive an allowance or are possibly even working? Money skills aren't a luxury—they're as essential as knowing how to read. So, if you're drowning in debt right now, maybe it's not your fault when you realize—no one ever taught you what the hell to do with your money. But to be a responsible adult, remember we do not blame others, although it's a disadvantage the system ill-prepared us for the real world; we are all in the same pot, so at some point, we have to take responsibility for our own lives because being a victim never wins. This means if we weren't guided by some money mentor, it's time to get self-taught. So congratulations if this is your 1st step!

We get erratically emotional about money because we don't understand it. And when we don't understand something, we fear it. We make odd, avoidant choices like ignoring our bank statements, stuffing our unopened bills into a drawer, or convincing ourselves that someone will come and save us. Spoiler Alert: No one is coming! No one. This battle is with you and you only. You can ignore it all you want, but it will seep into every aspect of your life until it's unmanageable. If you're ever going to get past our financial mishaps, you need to see that money isn't the enemy. Ignorance is. You can love money, respect money, and learn how to make more of it without turning into a soulless, Scrooge-y, dollar-hoarding monster.

Money isn't scary. Staying broke and confused about it is. Your financial future is in your hands, and the sooner you stop avoiding it, the sooner you can start creating wealth instead of just wishing for it. So that's why you started this book, to start making money moves, and it all starts with knowledge. Because here's the deal—you cannot afford (literally) to be financially illiterate. Ignoring money doesn't make it go away; it is like putting off going to the dentist until your toothache turns into a full-blown root canal.

But fear not, my friends. Money's just a tool, like a hammer, and it's about time we got comfortable with it. If we start yakkin' openly about our financial lives, we can kick that money talk taboo to the dumps, and soon, we'll all be chatting about our finances over brunch, like gabbing about our ex-lovers. Let's normalize money talk. Money, at its core, is a tool – a medium of exchange that facilitates transactions. It's neither inherently good nor evil but a reflection of our values and preferences. By engaging in open, non-judgmental conversations about money, we can break down the taboos, enhance our financial literacy, and better align our finances with our values and goals.

Money is often a topic we shy away from, fearing judgment or revealing too much. In understanding the reasons for our discomfort, we can start to reshape our perceptions of money, moving from a place of anxiety to one of empowerment. Our challenge is to move from silence to dialogue, from taboo to education, and from fear to understanding. It is then that we will truly harness the power of wealth, not as a judge of worth, but as a tool for creating a life of purpose and meaning.

To understand money, we first need to strip it of the emotional and societal baggage we often ascribe to it. The reality is this: money, in its essence, is neutral. It is a mere tool, a symbol for the exchange of goods and services. Money is paper. Paper is just the physical representation of money. It is nothing more than what we have crowned as symbols of value because unless you're using it to write your million-dollar business plan, it lacks any direct function. The standard paper currency operates in this conceptual realm, serving as an intermediary in a system of acknowledged worth. This piece of paper that we refer to as a "dollar" is quite literally labeled paper, to which we assign the meaning. You can eat a $100 bill, and it will not nourish you with food, shelter, or health. It cannot produce fruit or heal us of a disease. The agreement is that it can be exchanged for all of these items, services, and more. It has been granted the authority to exchange services and goods as a result of our collective agreement. Basically, if the government decided tomorrow, instead of paper money, we're switching to Pokemon cards, paper money would all be meaningless. The lesson here is to break the spell of glorifying money or chasing it. We first have to understand that money is neutral, and real security comes from your ability to create, give service, and connect with others.

Imagine if every time you wanted a pair of shoes, you had to track down a cobbler who just *happened* to be craving the bushel of apples you grew. Sounds exhausting, right? That's why paper money saved us from the chaotic mess of bartering, trading, and trying to convince someone that your goat is worth exactly three loaves of bread and a back massage. Instead of weighing gold like medieval treasure hunters or hiring a cow whisperer to determine if Bessie is worth a new iPhone, we just flash some paper (or tap a card) and boom—transaction complete. Thanks to this modern-day fiat system, we've built a global economy where you can buy sneakers from halfway across the world without ever having to negotiate livestock. At the end of the day, money is just a tool we invented to make life easier. It's not the goal—it's just the thing that helps you get the *actual* goal (which, let's be real, is probably tacos).

In its most basic form, money is a medium of exchange, enabling the exchange of commodities and services between parties. It is also a widely recognized symbol that aids in determining the worth of products and services, facilitating simpler and easier transactions. Money is a neutral instrument and resource; it is neither good nor harmful. Its importance, worth, and the consequences of its use are derived entirely from our intentions and actions.

It's erroneously believed that money is either intrinsically positive or negative. As a result, many people feel perplexed and disoriented when it comes to the idea of money. Money is merely a neutral tool. It is solely a tool, neither intrinsically moral nor immoral, just as water is a source of replenishment or a heavy storm. As impartial as the hammer that constructs or destroys a house and as unbiased as the water that satisfies thirst or inundates a community. Like water, money adopts the shape of the container it is poured into. The power of money transforms into a harmful force when we pour it into a vessel that has been fashioned by greed, corruption, or harm. If we pour it into a generously proportioned vessel shaped by generosity, kindness, or ambition, money becomes a force for good.

Imagine a hammer in your mind; the hammer could be used to create a refuge or commit vandalism. A moral compass is not present in the hammer. It is an instrument in the user's hands; the user's intentions and actions destine its function, not the hammer itself. This is similar to the fact that there is no morality in money. It adopts the personality of the person who owns it. It shines with kindness and service in Mother Teresa's hands. It turns into a device for deceit and manipulation when it's in the hands of a sinister person. Money stays the same, just a neutral tool. The individual using it determines whether it has a positive or negative influence. Its worth, meaning, and influence on how we use money are all products of our intentions and deeds. The purpose is determined by how we decide the usage of money, not the amount itself, which is what counts. The money myth of "money changes you" is false because it's not that it changes you; it just gives you more freedom and allows you to be more of who you are. Knowing this now, ask yourself, what kind of person do you aspire to be? What kind of rich person do you want to be? What kind of person are you now? How can you become your ideal self now?

Let's speculate on two situations. One on the one hand, a man buys drugs with a $100 bill, supporting bad habits and feeding the cycle of drug usage. On the other hand, a woman invests in education and nurtures her future by using the same 100 dollars to invest in her education. Our connection to money frequently reflects how we feel inside. Money becomes an accomplice to our vices if we are driven by greed and a desire for power. Money turns into a tool for virtue when compassion and service are our motivating factors. Just like how you would use a hammer, how would you use money? To build or destroy? You are making that decision with every dollar. Is it bringing you joy, or is it sabotaging your present or future reality?

Money can liberate or subjugate, create or destroy, heal or harm. However, this authority is held by us, not by money. By employing the tool of money and deciding where it should go, we can influence our lives and the world around us on a larger scale. But it begins with accepting its objectivity and realizing that its genuine worth is determined by our intentions and deeds, not based on its sole existence.

We must not let money be the lord of our lives. We are the captains of our lives and our finances. Money reflects our objectives and ideals as well as an extension of our will. If we decide to hoard, it represents avarice. If we decide to share, it becomes a sign of generosity.

Therefore, accepting money as a neutral force is the first step in developing a positive relationship with it. The second is realizing that money has meaning and power as a consequence of our actions and attitudes regarding how we use it, not the other way around.

When we accept these realities, we start down the path to abundance and freedom. This includes the intelligence to manage the world of financial possibilities without losing sight of our values and not just the capacity to earn and spend. This freedom comes from knowing who we are and being grounded in our values, not just from having more money.

So, let's dispel the myths and fallacies associated with money. Let's undo the ingrained beliefs that relate to having money with guilt, fear, or superiority. Let's see money for what it really is: a tool in the magician's hand that should only be used responsibly. You can change the world with your money and intention, one dollar at a time. Money travels with a neutral force, directed by the intentions of those who manage it with clarity, from the center of New York City to the far-flung villages of Africa, from the splendor of royal palaces to the simplicity of country farmhouses. Money does not discriminate; it is inherently a neutral force of energy.

10

Money is an Amplifier

Money isn't the big bad wolf. It's not waiting in the shadows to corrupt your soul or make you an insufferable snob. Money can be your best friend who's always got your back. It's an incredible resource that can change lives in the right hands. And those 'right hands' can be yours, too.

It's time to wash away all the dirt around your money, beliefs, and energy, blocking you from nature's waterfall of abundance. It's time to shift your perception of money towards the light: it's about the green-green fields, green trees, and green lights for your dreams. Money is like a seed. Nurture it will love, light, and good energy, and it will grow into a big ol' tree of possibilities. Because that one big tree you'll grow will produce more seeds for income streams, and soon you'll have an evergreen forest of multiple income streams leading to ultimate freedom. It's going to sprout more opportunities for growth and expansion, as well as the potential to change people's lives and the world on a greater scale.

The truth behind money holds an invaluable lesson to our relationship with money. Beneath the material surface of coin and paper, beneath the flickering numbers on digital screens, lies an undercurrent of profound psychological, spiritual, and moral implications. One such insight stands out among the rest: Money is an amplifier. It expands more of who you already are. It's a calling for introspection and a challenge to our identities, our values, and our motivations.

To begin with, it's essential to understand that money, in its purest form, is a neutral force, as benign as a seashell. The user's intention and character determine the nature of its application. Here, then, is where we encounter our first revelation: Money amplifies your existing characteristics, your inherent virtues, and your vices.

It's not the money that corrupts; it's the people who allow themselves to be corrupted. This is where we bust the myth that money is the root of all evil. That's like saying guitars are the root of all bad music. It's not the money or the guitar that's the problem; it's how it's used and the intention behind the use of money.

Money is not the core issue; it's who you are being and who you are becoming. Getting wealthy is becoming the kind of person who can handle it, grow it, and use it for something greater than yourself. That kind of transformation doesn't happen overnight, and it sure as hell doesn't happen by accident. That's why lottery winners don't actually win; it's about the journey to wealth. Your journey to becoming wealthy is where the magic happens—where you shed your excuses, toughen up your mindset, and step into the best version of yourself that is able to handle large sums of money. If you don't prepare by emotionally mastering your mind, body, & soul to be clear, safe, & stable with riches, it will exit your life as soon as it comes.

The process of building wealth is like boot camp for your soul. It forces you to say goodbye to every lazy, fearful, self-sabotaging version of yourself that's been holding you back. Procrastination? It crumbles under the weight of real opportunities. Impulsiveness? It gets its own by strategic thinking. Playing the victim? Sorry, but wealth doesn't do pity parties. The journey doesn't just suggest growth—it demands it.

You either level up or get left behind.

Financial success is never just about money. It's about who you become to earn it. The art of making money forces you to master skills you never thought you had—mastering your skills, discipline, risk-taking, emotional intelligence, and resilience. It pushes you to think big, take action, and step into your power. Every obstacle you face is a lesson. Every failure is a rite of passage. And every win? Proof that you are capable of so much more than you ever imagined.

Wealth-building has a way of exposing you—your habits, your beliefs, your relationships, and most importantly, your relationship with yourself. The market doesn't give a damn about your excuses. It rewards the ability to turn challenges into opportunities. The road to riches is paved with risk, rejection, and moments that will make you question everything. But here's the thing: fear is just an illusion. It's your mind's way of keeping you "safe," when in reality, it's keeping you small. Every time you push past fear—whether it's launching a business or investing in yourself—you expand your capacity for greatness.

Money doesn't change you. It amplifies who you already are. If you're a generous, visionary leader, wealth will make you unstoppable. If you're a hot mess who can't manage a budget, it'll just give you bigger problems. That's why the universe doesn't hand out wealth to people who aren't ready for it. When you expand yourself to be authentic and feel truly abundant in the energy of joy and gratitude, the Universe will resonate and reflect it back to you monetarily. But if you're resonating in fear and inauthenticity, then you are blocking the flow of money to you. This may explain why you might allow yourself to only receive the bare minimum just to get by. Your money consciousness has a certain limit based on your beliefs and emotions towards money. You have to expand your money consciousness to grow into the version of yourself who can handle riches and who can use it for something greater than yourself, which might even be to start a family.

At the end of the day, wealth isn't just about making money—it's about expanding your potential and making an impact. The real win is creating something valuable, solving problems, and leaving the world better than you found it. Wealth isn't about what you get; it's about who you become and what you contribute.

Picture a philanthropist who receives a large sum of money. With this influx, they don't become greedy or self-serving. Instead, they expand their altruism, increasing their charitable donations and creating more opportunities for those less fortunate. They use the money to amplify their inherent desire to help and contribute to society.

Now, consider someone driven by greed and selfishness. When they acquire wealth, it's not used to benefit others. Instead, it becomes a tool for further self-aggrandizement, amplifying their insatiable desires. Money does not corrupt them; they are already leaning towards avarice and egocentrism.

You have the choice to do what you want with your money. Money can be a force for unbelievable good, like Oprah or Elon Musk. They used their fortunes to make massive waves of change. Money can expand the power of your personal impact on people and the world.

The beauty and the beast of money lie in this amplification effect. It's like an enhancer that brings out more of what's already within us. Hence, it is of the utmost importance that we introspect and identify the traits we carry within us. Are they virtues or vices we want to amplify? How much self-control do you have? You have the choice to do what you want with your money. You can be the humanitarian, the best parent, help the underprivileged, or the next Elon Musk, fueling the next big innovation. Claim your riches if your heart is good because we need more good in this world to combat all the misfortunes of this world. It's about spreading goodness to the world and expanding humanity with your personal impact. Money can do good, and lots of it.

To be a money magnet, you have to expand your money consciousness.

Money flows as a response to our state of being. The cosmos operates with profound intelligence, distributing abundance not by chance but through the precise mechanism of energetic resonance. This understanding reveals why true wealth arrives only when we've developed the consciousness to steward it wisely.

Consider the universe an infinite mirror, reflecting back the exact frequency of our inner state. When we vibrate at the frequency of lack, scarcity, and fear, these limitations manifest in our financial reality. Our money consciousness—the sum of our beliefs, emotions, and attitudes about wealth—creates an energetic ceiling that determines the level of abundance we're capable of receiving.

The journey to expanding our money consciousness begins with a fundamental shift in our way of being. It's not about forcing or chasing but about allowing ourselves to expand into authenticity. When we align with our true purpose and operate from a place of genuine joy and gratitude, we naturally elevate our energetic frequency to match that of abundance itself.

Fear and inauthenticity act as energetic barriers, blocking the natural flow of wealth. These lower-frequency states create resistance in our energy field, preventing us from receiving the abundance that constantly seeks expression through us. This explains why many find themselves trapped in cycles of barely getting by—their consciousness has set a limit based on deep-seated beliefs about what they deserve or can handle.

The universe responds not to our wants but to our energetic state of being. Money, in its essence, resonates with the frequency of freedom. When we align with our soul's purpose and allow ourselves to be guided by authentic joy, we naturally match this frequency. Think about when you are doing something you love; you are in the energy field of joy, creativity, and freedom. You're not bogged down by thinking of your next paycheck or bill due dates, which lowers your energy to fear. Your mind and energy expand when you do something you love because, essentially, you are in the energy of love. This alignment creates an energetic opening through which abundance can flow freely.

Following our heart's wisdom and pursuing what ignites our soul is a pathway to opening our vessel for divine purpose—plus, it's a practical pathway to expanding our capacity for abundance. As we honor our true calling, we experience a natural expansion of consciousness that attracts supporting resources, opportunities, and abundance. The universe conspires in our favor through the natural law of resonance. Synchronicities are a way to witness signs that you are on the right path.

Our authentic purpose serves as a gateway to higher states of consciousness. When we fully commit to this path, we activate the divine potential within ourselves. This activation raises our energetic frequency, allowing us to become natural conduits for greater levels of abundance. The key lies in pursuing our divine calling with such wholehearted dedication that abundance becomes a natural byproduct of our expanded state of being.

Expanding our money consciousness requires us to release old patterns of thinking and feeling about wealth. These limitations, often inherited or unconsciously adopted, must be recognized and transformed. As we elevate our consciousness through authentic living and purposeful action, we naturally outgrow these constraints, allowing new levels of abundance to flow into our experience.

True abundance follows emotional mastery. When we liberate ourselves from the fear-based patterns that kept us small, we create space for prosperity to enter. This liberation comes through embracing our authentic path, allowing joy to be our guide, and trusting in the universal principles that govern abundance.

Each step taken in alignment with our heart's wisdom creates ripples in the fabric of reality. These ripples return to us as synchronicities, opportunities, and resources that support our journey. The universe's response to our authentic expression isn't random—it's a precise reflection of our expanded consciousness.

The path to greater abundance requires alignment—the alignment to be authentically ourselves, to follow our unique calling, and to allow ourselves to receive more than we previously thought possible. As we develop this alignment, we naturally expand our capacity to receive and maintain higher levels of abundance.

By understanding these universal principles, we can consciously participate in the flow of abundance. Rather than struggling against the current, we learn to align ourselves with the natural expansion that occurs when we live our truth. This alignment creates an upward spiral where increased authenticity leads to greater abundance, which in turn supports further expansion of consciousness.

Our relationship with money transforms when we recognize it as a form of energy that responds to our state of being. By focusing on expanding our consciousness through authentic living and purposeful action, we naturally attract the level of wealth that matches our expanded state. The key lies not in chasing money but in becoming the person whose natural vibration attracts abundance with alignment to their divine purpose.

Money provides an amplification, a wider platform, and a broader stage for these elements to expand. Money is like a loudspeaker for your soul. It gives freedom and the opportunity to be more, do more, and give more.

What can we take away from this understanding? First, a reframed relationship with money. It's neither a devil to be shunned nor a god to be worshiped. It's an amplifier, a tool, and like any tool, its efficacy and morality depend on the user.

Second, it is a call to self-awareness and personal growth. If money amplifies who we are, we must become the best versions of ourselves, embodying virtues like kindness, empathy, and integrity. That way, when we do acquire wealth, we become benefactors, not malefactors.

Third, expand your wealth consciousness by living in alignment with authenticity and your divine purpose. With emotional mastery and feelings of love and joy, the universe will meet you halfway with possibilities that conspire in your favor. You will become a natural money magnet.

Lastly, money can be a powerful force for good, amplifying positive change. Wealthy philanthropists who have used their fortunes to benefit humanity exemplify a testament to the positive potential of money.

In the end, we need to remember that money is a reflection and extension of our inner selves, a metaphysical magnifier that reveals who we truly are. By viewing it as such, we can transform our relationship with money into one of conscious intention and purposeful utilization.

11

Money Mirrors Your Values

Money is a reflection of our values. Look at your most current bank and credit card statements on paper. Review every single purchase and categorize them. What percentage of your spending is on necessities such as rent, groceries, car, etc.? What percentage of your spending is on entertainment, personal care, shopping, etc.? Aside from your necessity categories, how much extra spending money do you have for yourself? What do you spend it on? How much do you save? It's time to confront your finances and be honest with the results of your financial spending. Analyze every purchase and connect each one to reflect one of your values.

Money Values:

1. **Financial Security:** Many people prioritize financial security, which means they focus on saving money, building an emergency fund, and avoiding unnecessary debt.
2. **Sustainability:** Some individuals value sustainability and environmentally friendly practices. They may spend more on eco-friendly products and support businesses with sustainable practices.

3. **Health and Well-being:** People who prioritize health and well-being may be willing to spend more on quality food, fitness, and healthcare to maintain a healthy lifestyle.

4. **Education:** Education is often highly valued, and people may allocate a significant portion of their budget to support learning opportunities for themselves.

5. **Experiences:** Some individuals prefer spending on experiences, such as travel, concerts, or cultural events.

6. **Family and Relationships:** Family-oriented individuals may prioritize spending on activities and items that strengthen family bonds and relationships.

7. **Community and Charity:** Those who value community and charitable giving may allocate funds to support local organizations or causes they care about.

8. **Quality and Longevity:** Some people prioritize purchasing high-quality, durable products, even if they are more expensive upfront, as they may last longer and provide better value in the long run.

9. **Personal Growth:** Some individuals value personal development and growth, which may lead them to spend money on courses, workshops, or self-improvement resources.

10. **Aesthetics and Beauty:** People who value aesthetics and appearance may spend on beauty products, clothing, or home decor to enhance their surroundings and self-image.

11. **Convenience:** Convenience can be a significant factor in spending decisions. Some individuals may prioritize time-saving services or products even if they come at a higher cost.

12. **Insert your own personal values from here.**

If there are values not listed above that are important to you, make sure to write them down. According to your bank statements, what do your expenses represent in terms of your values? Are you spending most of your money on experiences? Maybe one of your values is having fun or spending quality time with your friends and family. Only you can speculate and explain what your expenses reflect and which values they mean for you. The outgoing expenses only log which category it applies to, and then you have to make the connection to how it reflects your personal value. Sometimes, spending more on convenience means you value your time. Sometimes, your spending can be a little more complicated and not so straightforward, such as emotional spending, impulsive purchases, unexpected expenses, etc. It's important not to jump to judgments and view this entire exercise as a health examination for your financial health.

Some people view money as a tool for security, while others see it as a means to enjoy life to the fullest. The trick is balancing your checkbook for both. Understanding your money attitude can help you make more conscious spending decisions. We often hear the phrase, "Show me your bank statements, and I'll show you your priorities." Money is more than numbers on a page; it carries the imprints of our behaviors, emotions, and, most importantly, our values. Every financial decision we make, consciously or unconsciously, is influenced by our core beliefs and values.

Think about the last significant expense you made. Was it a spontaneous indulgence or a conscious investment in something that aligns with your long-term vision? By exploring the genesis of these spending decisions, we begin to unravel the profound connection between our values and our money. Sometimes, we say we value our future well-being and want to retire as a millionaire, but what does our bank statement say? Are you spending towards your future through education, investments, or savings? If a bank teller were to read each line of purchase from your bank statement out loud to you, in person, face-to-face, what would you come to realize? There's a reason why your bank statements are so personal. Whether we are aware of our spending habits or not, our bank statements are receipts of our values at that moment of spending. They reflect our priorities and values at a given moment in time. Forget what you *say* you value—your bank statements are the hard facts. They're the unfiltered truth serum of your life, laying bare what you actually care about, whether you are aware of it or not.

Think of your finances as a mirror—one that doesn't sugarcoat a damn thing. It reflects *all* your choices: the late-night Amazon binges, the gym membership you never use, the investments (or lack thereof), the organic groceries, the designer handbag, the charity donations, etc. This mirror is just a reflection. It doesn't judge. It just reflects. And if you have the guts to really *look* at it, you'll gain some serious insights about yourself—some inspiring, some surprising, and some that might make you cringe.

For example, let's say you claim, "Health is my #1 priority!" You can declare to the world that health is your top priority, but if your credit card statement is a graveyard of fast-food receipts and abandoned gym memberships, your money is calling your bluff. You can chant morning and night that financial independence is your goal, but if your spending habits scream, "I can't say no to a flash sale," then guess what? Your wallet knows the real you. Seeing the gaps between what you claim to value and where your money actually goes isn't about shame—it's about self-awareness, and that's the first step to change, to give you a chance to align your actions to your values.

Your spending habits also reveal your mindset about *time*—which is actually your most precious (and non-refundable) resource. If you regularly invest in books, courses, therapy, or wellness, you're making a clear statement that your future self matters. But if your money mostly goes toward instant gratification—daily lattes, impulse buys, streaming subscriptions—you might be operating under an unconscious response in either escaping current reality or satiating an indulgence. Neither approach is "right" nor "wrong," but knowing *why* you spend the way you do and being self-aware is where the money consciousness is in action. If we aren't checking and reflecting on our finances, we forget about that one late-night delivery enough to feed small farm animals because we were going through a breakup.

Don't let fear lead your finances. Have you ever met someone who insists they want financial freedom but won't give up their expensive but miserable lifestyle? Fear shows up in *all* kinds of ways—overspending, avoiding financial conversations, or hoarding free ketchup packets. If your spending habits scream "people-pleaser" with a side of "fear of missing out," maybe it's time to ask yourself whose life you're financing—yours or everyone else's? The key is recognizing when your spending is driven by fear instead of purpose.

So, what's the takeaway? Awareness. Once you *see* what your financial mirror is reflecting, you can start making conscious choices instead of running on autopilot. Want to be a person who values health? Start investing in it. Want to be someone who prioritizes relationships? Spend on experiences with the people you enjoy being with. Want to support ethical businesses? Redirect your dollars to companies that align with your causes. Your money is a tool—wield it like an architect designing the life you *actually* want instead of unconsciously makeshifting one that ends up causing chaos.

Sometimes, you'll spend in ways that seem out of alignment with your values, and that's okay—as long as it's ideally less than 10% of the time. We want to keep the percentage as low as possible. The goal isn't perfection; it's keeping your mistakes *minimal*. Of course, you're allowed some ice cream here and there, just not every day! Intentional indulgence is different than unconscious spending. The key is awareness. Every time you're aware, you strengthen your sense of self. You prove to yourself that you're in charge of your money— not the other way around. At the end of the day, your expenses are a reflection of your priorities and values at that current moment in time, and sometimes, it is just about enjoying the simple things of a hot new latte in town.

Now that you've gained a deeper understanding of your spending and values and how they intertwine with your financial health, it's time to become a money magnet. Getting clear with your values, you are now equipped to make more informed and empowered financial decisions with self-awareness. Remember, managing money is not just about numbers; it's about understanding your values and using that insight to make conscious decisions. Make every dollar work for you—whether it's building your savings or investing in that therapist who promises to fix your entire life.

12

Poverty is Pain

Living paycheck to paycheck is like living in a fortress of anxiety that's got your well-being held hostage. Covered with piles of towering bills that bring a chronic state of perpetual dread that is slowly grinding you down in every way, mentally, psychologically, emotionally, & physically. You're not just paying with money you don't have — you're paying with your life force, your zest for life, your mental well-being & physical wellness.

In a society steeped in a relentless pursuit of wealth and power, a silent, pervasive force lies at the heart of many individuals' ability to ascend to unparalleled prosperity. This force, ever-constant yet amorphous, restricts a vast number of people from engaging in wealth-building activities, locking them in an unforgiving cycle of attending to their immediate survival needs. The great strategist Sun Tzu once emphasized the cunning tactic of encircling one's enemy, sapping them of their resources and will until they are rendered helpless. The phenomenon we explore in this chapter examines poverty tightening its grip on individuals, and squeezing the vigor and vitality needed for the visionary pursuits of abundance and greatness for every soul.

In the unseen realms of our world, a spiritual battle perpetually rages—a conflict between forces of light and shadow, love and fear. This dichotomy, deeply entrenched in the sacred wisdom of the ancients and reverberating through the corridors of contemporary metaphysics, manifests as the Law of Polarity. It is a universal principle stating that all things have their opposing force. Just as the darkness of night inevitably surrenders to the dawn's light, and the ocean's tides rise and fall in eternal rhythm, so too does every facet of our existence dance to this eternal waltz of dualities.

Our sacred journey on this earthly plane, this divine assignment, is to ascend towards ever-higher echelons of expansion. This world, intricately woven with threads of polarity and contrast, serves as the human experience for our spiritual evolution. Here, the dual energies of love and fear perpetually orbit our lives, vying for our attention. But amidst this cosmic tug-of-war, we are endowed with a precious gift— the power of choice. At any given moment, we stand at the crossroads between love and fear. Awareness becomes our lantern in this journey, illuminating the truth that fears often clamors for our attention with its cacophonous roar while love whispers its wisdom in the serene stillness of our inner being. It is imperative, then, to attune to our higher selves, making choices that resonate with the harmonious frequency of love that is akin to the Source, Universe, & higher forces, including angels, etc.

Just as the energy of love has a feeling of pure divine light, there is an opposite force of dark energy that manifests as fear. Envision fear as a tyrannical ruler, Mr.Evil, devoid of your best interests, scheming tirelessly to erode your light and psychological fortitude, seeking dominion over your spirit. Such a regime would first strip away the power of knowledge, ensuring that critical thinking remains distant, blocking you from even first being aware. Reflect, for instance, on the plight of poverty, where the lack of financial literacy is a critical barrier. The teachings of money management, conspicuously absent from our educational institutions and often unspoken of in homes, remain elusive to many, perpetuating a cycle of economic disenfranchisement.

Money, that most tangible measure of earthly value, circulates as the lifeblood of our daily existence. It's an exchange for essentials like nourishment, shelter, attire, and healthcare. Yet, astonishingly, within the halls of our educational institutions, not a whisper is spoken about its nature or management. We traverse through formative years without a single lesson on saving, investing, or the art of financial stewardship. For those without family guidance or mentors to illuminate the path of fiscal wisdom, the journey becomes a trek through the uncharted wilderness, guided only by the unexamined beliefs and patterns absorbed by our subconscious minds.

In this void of financial education, our relationship with money often morphs into an emotional labyrinth. Within many households, money either looms as a source of perpetual strife or dwells as a topic shrouded in silence. Meanwhile, the incessant barrage of marketing and consumerist culture diverts our attention, leading us astray from strategic money management. In today's world, where we're all glued to our screens, we're constantly advertising these distractions that lure us away from a path of financial integrity.

This is how Dr. Evil keeps you trapped, ensnaring us in a web of material bondage. The first thread is woven through the deprivation of knowledge, leaving us unarmed in the face of life's financial complexities. Ignorance becomes the chain that binds our potential. Next, this cunning force inundates our senses with the relentless allure of materialism, bombarding us with messages that equate worth with possessions, thus diverting us from our true path to personal fulfillment. We are seduced into a world where the acquisition of things overshadows the cultivation of our inner selves.

Then, we find ourselves entrapped in a vicious cycle of debt, lured by the deceptive temporary glittery instant gratification of credit cards.

Unaware of the fine print that speaks of compounding interest rates, we unwittingly bind ourselves to a relentless pursuit of keeping up with societal benchmarks of success, embodied by the proverbial 'Joneses.' This pursuit, hollow and unfulfilling, steers us further away from our authentic selves.

Finally, we are shackled to jobs that drain our spirit, jobs that are far removed from our true calling, all in an effort to satiate the endless demands of our accumulated debts. Trapped in this cycle, we lead lives that are but a shadow of our true potential, constantly haunted by the nagging question, "Is this all there is?"

Dr. Evil traps you into poverty, where an individual's primary objective centers on survival. Food, shelter, warmth—basic human needs to take precedence. Eventually, the chains of immediate needs begin to tighten, stifling any ambition that dares to look beyond the pressing demands of present survival needs.

In this vortex of poverty, individuals find themselves consumed by relentless urgencies, drowned in debts, burdened by familial obligations, and gripped by fears that render them unable to even contemplate wealth-building activities. They are entrapped in a hamster wheel of survival, their energies sucked dry by the unyielding demands of the present moment, leaving no room for the cultivation of assets that could construct a prosperous future.

Being poor is more expensive. You are not just scrambling to make ends meet, but you are caught in a storm of higher interest rates, premium fees, and the vicious cycle of living in scarcity and fear every day. It's more than financial; it's a tax on your dreams, your creativity, and your opportunities.

Being poor causes stress and takes a toll on your mentality and health. Your body reacts to being constantly hypervigilant; it revolts with a cocktail of stress hormones that can spiral into chronic health conditions. Next thing you know, you're piling up with medical debts, but remember, warrior, even in the battleground, there is an oasis of well-being, and it starts with creating an action plan out of this cycle of poverty with resilience and determination.

This collective quandary, this pervasive ignorance regarding the essence and handling of money, is not merely a coincidence but a systemic flaw—a testament to a foundational failure in our upbringing and education. We find ourselves adrift in a sea of economic uncertainty, not by chance but by a designed omission in our learning, leaving us ill-prepared to navigate the financial realities of our world. It is a predicament that beckons for awakening and transformation, urging us to seek knowledge and empowerment in this crucial aspect of our lives.

Although this system doesn't prepare us for success, blaming or resorting to victimhood is not the answer. To unravel the enigma of "how did you get here?" it is crucial to note that Mr. Evil has gatekept wealth from you through a smokescreen of ignorance, and it's time to clear that barrier with some truth. The opposite force of this Dr.Evil is the power of love, the source of the Universe, pure divine light. How do you choose love in this predicament of fear?

In these moments, it is essential to pause and broaden our perspective, moving beyond the limited view of our own experience to a broader, more expanded vantage point, akin to that of a satellite orbiting in space, where we are a speck of sand in comparison to the size of the whole Universe. There's a far greater force out there, beyond the star-studded galaxies known as *the Universe*, that operates in divine perfection. Just remember there exists a higher force known as the Universe, overseeing everything from the star systems in space to the wild waves of the oceans and everything under the sun; every piece of nature, including those eccentric tiny seahorses, is all part of nature's grand design—espccially the one and only you!

The Universe is a higher divine intelligent force engineering all the systems of life, with a perfection beyond our understanding. Let's reference this divine energy as "The Universe," "The Source," or "Pure Divine Light" – whichever one you resonate with best, call it whatever you'd like. This higher power represents a sublime order, reminding us that we're all part of something far greater with a divine purpose and plan if we choose to flow with it. Beyond living consumed with the inner anxieties of our day-to-day lives lies an outer vast magical multiverse beyond earth, the sun, and the far distant planets. There's a greater force at play here, and this force represents divine perfection. Knowing this truth is the key to the path of our inner innate abundance.

Need proof? Just step outside. There is evidence of its divinity all around us, and we just take it for granted because we're so consumed with what other people think about us and care too much about minuscule shenanigans. We're busy hustling to keep up with the Joneses and, of course, all the drama, drama, drama in our lives, following our favorite true crime series, the news, and on and on. We take nature for granted and get jaded by the grandiosity of the universe. But if you focus on the miracle of life, you will soon believe that life is a miracle every day. Spend a day alone in solitude and marvel at how beautiful flowers can bloom just from a tiny seed, how a humble acorn could grow into a massive towering oak tree, listen to the birds singing nature's concertos, and watch squirrels as they unwittingly mastermind where to plant their treasured acorns. Did you know that half the time, these little nut bandits forget where they squirreled their nutty treasures? That's how trees are planted! This is the Universe's divine interplay—apparent chaos with an underlying order, the divine inner workings of the Universe. There's a method to this kind of madness, even if it appears as chaos. And that's life's journey in a nutshell; there are "nuts" being planted everywhere at all times, and we just don't know yet how it will all manifest in the grand design of life. Life is a continual planting of 'seeds' through our choices, shaping the grand design of our futures. Only with time and nurturing the garden of our mind and spirit do we see the fruits of our labor. That's our life on the individual level as well; we're just planting seeds every day, at every moment, and every second of our lives with every single decision we make, which creates the grand design of our lives. We can only see the fruits of our labor after many seasons of tending to the garden of our mind and spirit with consistent nurture. Every aspect of our well-being—mental, physical, emotional, social, spiritual, personal, professional, financial—is interconnected, requiring care to flourish and thrive. Behind the veil, the Universe is the master architect of life's happenings. Each of us is a vital part of nature's ecosystem, intertwined within society's network. Behind everything, there is a connection, a purpose, an interwoven tapestry of every soul encounter and experience.

So why all the yammering about the Universe and its divine perfection, you ask? You see when we're knee-deep in crap, we forget about all the wonder and magic that life has to offer. Your financial woes are like a starved vampire that's taking a bite out of your bloodline, sucking up all your energy and spirit, reducing you to a terrified heap with night sweats. When we're drowning in a financial storm, it's hard to see beyond the sea of red. It's emotionally, psychologically, & physically draining where we lose hope, faith, & motivation. But remember, this is just a temporary season of your life, and this, too, shall pass. It's just a lesson that the Universe is delivering to you, wrapped in the form of a life-altering experience.

If there is such a thing as perfect, we could all agree that maybe the one thing would be the Universe, the Source of all life. The Universe organizes all of the cosmos and all of human life, and it's a higher intelligent force that is the original source of everything and the architect of everything in all dimensions. We can all agree that the only entity we can call perfect is "God" (whatever that means to you: Spirit, Jesus, Buddha, Angels, etc.) Here, we'll refer to it as *The Universe/Source.* It's a higher-intelligent force with infinite energy, potential, intelligence, and unconditional love. This force, characterized by infinite energy, divine intelligence, and unconditional love, encompasses all knowledge and is omnipresent, with a direct line to human consciousness and beyond. It operates with a focus on the greater good, ensuring the best outcomes. Remember, the Universe is an ally, aligning with those who hold pure intentions. The Universe only operates through the lens of unconditional love. Maintain faith and trust that everything aligns for your highest good and the collective good. There is a divine grand plan behind the veil of our earthly life experience.

Life is still about experiencing contrast. We still suffer from human problems even though we are spiritual beings. Before entering this earth realm, our spirits desired to experience the entire human experience of living on 3D earth, which means experiencing contrast to understand the whole. Sometimes, we're in the dark for a season, but primarily for a reason. Your life experiences are all happening for a reason, and the Universe is always there to guide and support you along your journey to help you grow and expand to your highest version of yourself. Beyond our physical body lies our soul, spirit, and life force energy. This spirit chose to experience life in the material form to experience life on planet Earth as a human being. We can experience the simple pleasures of smelling roses, seeing the sunrise, and feeling all the intricacies of human emotions. Sometimes, to know great love, we first have to experience heartbreak. That is the reason for the contrast in our lives; it teaches us great life lessons so our souls can ascend to higher consciousness. Life's contrasts teach us valuable lessons, enriching our wisdom and elevating our consciousness. Experiencing contrast is like eating instant ramen every day and then being able to appreciate that gourmet lobster meal - the contrast makes the experience more enjoyable.

Life experiences are our chances for our human experiences to respond and exercise our free will. For it is in choosing love over fear that we find our liberation. Love, in its most profound essence, is synonymous with abundance. It radiates generosity, sharing its light freely, while fear lurks in the corners of selfishness and isolation. This 'Mr. Evil' epitomizes the shadow of greed, hoarding the wisdom of wealth, clinging to it as a miser with his gold. In stark contrast, love operates in the realm of a giving spirit and expansion, disseminating all forms of abundance like seeds in a fertile field, nurturing growth in a collective garden of prosperity.

Love recognizes that the universe's bounty is not a finite pie to be divided but an infinite spectrum of possibility, ample enough for all. In this spirit, love champions the belief that everyone deserves a place at the table of prosperity, where abundance creates more abundance. It is through this lens of love that we begin to see wealth not to be gripped so tightly but as a garden to be cultivated, a place where each of us can grow, flourish, and thrive together in harmony, where there's plenty of overflow for all. It's time we all start living like we are meant to because, in this universe, everyone deserves to be the main character in their own movie.

In the divine economy, there is no scarcity. Your receiving abundance doesn't diminish anyone else's supply. This belief is a distortion of divine truth. The universe is an ever-expanding field of energy, constantly creating, replenishing, and amplifying. In fact, when you allow yourself to receive fully, you enhance the flow of abundance for everyone around you. Your prosperity becomes an inspiration, a testament to what's possible when we align with our true worth.

When you thrive, you become a living testament to what is possible. Your success does not cast a shadow; it shines a light. Think of how seeing someone else achieve their dreams can inspire you to pursue your own. When you allow yourself to prosper, you pave the way for others to follow with inspiration.

Rather than feeling guilt over your blessings, ask yourself: How can my abundance create more abundance for others? A financially prosperous person can invest in businesses, create jobs, and support charitable causes. A joyful person can spread light to those around them, shifting the energy of an entire space. A wise leader can mentor others, multiplying wisdom through generations. Your abundance is not just for you; it is a ripple effect that impacts the lives you touch. Think of all the ways you can make a difference as your abundance grows. As you rise, you lift others and thrive together.

Abundance is an energy, a frequency, a way of being. When you cultivate abundant energy, you begin to radiate a magnetic force that attracts more of what your energy states. Imagine abundance as a flowing river—when you align yourself with its current, it naturally carries you to greater opportunities, abundance, and joy.

Wealthy individuals who understand abundance continue to generate more wealth because they believe in its limitless nature. They invest, they give, they expand. They do not hoard out of fear but circulate & participate in the flow of the economy, knowing that money is an energy that must flow to grow. Love operates the same way. Those who give love freely without fearing its depletion experience an overflow of love in return. The more you share, the more you receive. The world reflects your inner state—when you believe in limitless possibilities, they reveal themselves to you.

Conversely, lack is a bottomless pit that consumes everything in its path. It is not merely the absence of resources but a mindset that breeds limitation, fear, and scarcity. Those who believe they never have enough—be it money, love, opportunities, or happiness—unknowingly reinforce their own struggles.

Lack is a self-fulfilling prophecy. When you operate from fear of not having enough, you tighten your grip, resist change, and shrink from opportunities. You see competition instead of collaboration, obstacles instead of possibilities, and misfortune instead of blessings. Lack breeds negative energy, and negative energy repels success. Just as abundance multiplies itself, scarcity attracts more scarcity.

Scarcity is an illusion born from fear. It is the belief that there is not enough—whether it be love, money, success, or opportunity—to go around. This belief creates competition, hoarding, and a deep-seated anxiety about the future. But just as the sun does not ration its light, the divine flow of abundance does not restrict itself to a chosen few. The more we recognize that there is an inexhaustible supply available to all, the more we can shift from fear to love and from constriction to expansion.

Your brain is constantly bombarded with stressors that create a narrative of scarcity, fear, and lack. It's time to start rewriting your story with a vocabulary of abundance and fierce determination to conquer the mental circus of fears and anxiety. It is time to focus your mind intently on your dreams and to see barriers as mere speed bumps, not stop signs.

The key to unlocking divine abundance lies in recognizing your inherent worth. The universe does not measure deservingness the way society does. It does not ask for credentials, status, or permission slips. It simply responds to energy. When you align with the truth that you are already enough, already worthy, already a vessel of infinite potential, you remove the barriers that block the flow of abundance.

Become your higher self, and break free from this fortress of fears because the world is waiting to be impacted by your authentic higher self & the gifts you have to share with the world. Practice gratitude, love, and faith in the Universe. Release the belief that wealth, success, or fulfillment are external things you must chase. Instead, recognize that they are states of being that you cultivate from within. When you embody abundance, it manifests effortlessly in your life.

13

Ignorance is Not Bliss

In today's fast-paced and ever-changing world, the subject of money has become a puzzling enigma for countless individuals. It is not uncommon to witness anxiety-stricken humans burdened by the weight of financial uncertainty. People feel lost and overwhelmed when faced with the complexities of finance, often unsure where to begin or how to progress. The consequences of this lack of knowledge about money are far-reaching, affecting not only our personal finances but also those of younger generations, communities, and societies at large.

Imagine for a moment a master artisan, a sculptor who carves magnificent sculptures from rough stones. The artisan's skill and expertise did not emerge overnight but were the product of years of learning, practice, and a willingness to embrace mistakes as stepping stones toward mastery. Similarly, money is an art form, one that can be honed and perfected over time. Just as the artisan chisels away at imperfections, we, too, can chip away at our financial insecurities by recognizing that money is a skill that can be learned.

The key to unlocking the true potential of money lies in attaining financial literacy. Just as language is the foundation of communication, understanding financial concepts forms the bedrock of financial well-being. Financial literacy enables us to speak the language of money fluently, allowing us to manage our finances with confidence and clarity. Just as you wouldn't strut into a foreign country without knowing a lick of the language, you shouldn't dive into the realm of finance without your financial vocab down, too.

At its core, financial literacy encompasses a broad spectrum of knowledge. From basic budgeting skills to more advanced concepts like investing and managing debt, each piece contributes to the complete puzzle of financial success. Armed with this understanding, we are empowered to make informed decisions that align with our long-term goals and financial aspirations.

As with any skill worth mastering, education is the gateway to monetary well-being. Embracing a mindset of constant learning allows us to navigate the labyrinth of finance with greater ease. While the formal education system often fails to adequately prepare us for the real-world challenges of managing money, there are countless resources available to us in the age of the internet. Books, online courses, workshops, and more serve as valuable guides along this financial education journey. With this comprehension, we're poised to make judicious choices that resonate with our long-term visions and dreams. You're sculpting your dream life, one dollar at a time.

However, education alone is not enough; we must also put our knowledge into practice. Just as a musician improves through hours of dedicated practice, we, too, must apply financial concepts in our lives to reinforce our understanding and build financial resilience.

A true master never stops learning. As we develop our financial literacy and apply it to our lives, we must also embrace the concept of continuous improvement. The financial landscape is ever-changing, and to stay ahead, we must adapt and evolve with it.

Consider the seasoned sailor navigating stormy seas. To master the art of sailing, they must learn to adjust their course in response to the changing winds and tides. Similarly, our financial journey may encounter unforeseen challenges. By maintaining an open mind to navigate unpredictable events and a willingness to grow, we can weather any financial storm that comes our way with preparation.

The art of money mastery is within the grasp of every one of us. By acknowledging that money is a skill to be learned, we free ourselves from the shackles of financial anxiety. Financial literacy acts as the key to unlocking our potential, enabling us to navigate the complexities of finance with confidence and wisdom.

Education and practice form the building blocks of our financial knowledge, empowering us to make informed decisions that propel us toward our long-term goals. And just as master artisan refines their craft over time, continuous improvement ensures that we stay ahead of the curve, no matter the challenges we face.

Ignorance is not bliss on this journey of money mastery. Arm yourself with financial knowledge and continuous learning in the financial field, and you will be happier that you know what you are doing. Just like your physical health needs to be maintained, your financial health also needs the same amount of care and attention for a life of financial freedom and abundance.

14

Long-Term Wealth

In this chaotic world of lightning-fast modern living, our relationship with money holds the power to bring immense joy, comfort, and liberating freedom, but it can also become a source of stress, anxiety, and remorse. Far too often, our emotions dictate our financial choices, luring us into perilous paths of impulsive spending and unhealthy money decisions. Yet, fear not, for the key to genuine financial stability and success lies in mastering the art of emotional equilibrium around money.

Venturing into this transformative journey starts with comprehending the psychology behind our intimate connection with money. Throughout history, humans have woven intricate emotional threads around money, intertwining it with notions of security, success, and self-worth. These deep emotional ties can cloud our judgment and prompt irrational financial decisions. To break free from this hold, we must first recognize that money is simply a tool—a valuable instrument—but never a measure of our intrinsic value as unique individuals.

Before delving into the techniques that will bring about newfound stability in your emotions about money, the foundation must be built upon through self-awareness. Take a moment to reflect upon your past financial choices and unearth patterns of emotional spending or impulsive purchases. Identify the emotions triggering such behaviors — be it stress, boredom, fomo, or the yearning for validation. By understanding these emotional triggers, you pave the way to preemptively shield yourself against potential spending traps.

In a world of immediate gratification and tantalizing temptations, mastering the art of delayed gratification can be a game-changer. Train yourself to resist impulsive buying by implementing a cooling-off period before making significant purchases. Establish a personal rule: for any non-essential expense, grant yourself the gift of time at least 24 hours before committing. During this crucial interlude, reconsider your genuine necessity and the long-term impact of the purchase. More often than not, you will find yourself making wiser and more fulfilling choices.

Remember, stabilizing your emotions about money is not a fleeting destination but rather an enriching journey that demands self-awareness, determination, and practice. By realigning your core values, embracing the art of delayed gratification, and nurturing mindfulness with money, you can seize back control over your financial decisions. This path to financial triumph may not always be a smooth ride, but with steadfast emotional equilibrium, you can deftly navigate past spending traps and chart your course toward a future that is both secure and prosperous. Witness how mastering your emotions will set you on a course toward personal and financial freedom.

Imagine you've got grand visions of your future financial abundance - a life of ease and freedom where you can chase your dreams freely. But then, the allure of immediate pleasures pulls you away from your long-term goals. Those extravagant dinners, impulsive buys, and luxurious splurges may satisfy your feelings momentarily, but they create a conflict with your greater aspirations. It all comes down to one pivotal force: the mighty power of willpower.

Willpower is the invisible dynamo that propels us toward our dreams and brings positive change into our lives. It's that unyielding determination that carries us forward, even when we're confronted with challenges and temptations. Imagine it as a muscle that can be strengthened with dedicated practice. The more you work it out, the mightier it becomes and the greater impact it will have on your financial journey.

However, willpower needs the loyal companion of discipline to bridge the gap between your dreams and reality. Discipline is the art of making consistent choices that align with your financial values and purpose. It means setting up a budget, reigning in impulsive spending, and staying steadfast to your financial plan, no matter the distractions and temptations.

Take notes from the triumphs of successful investors and entrepreneurs who credit their prosperity to disciplined financial habits. They possess a relentless focus on their goals, sidestep emotional decision-making, and maintain patience during market fluctuations.

In our age of instant gratification, building wealth faces a daunting challenge. The allure of quick rewards can deviate us from our long-term objectives, leading to regrets and missed opportunities. The key lies in recognizing and managing these desires of instant gratification to construct sustainable wealth. Practice the art of delayed gratification in small ways, like avoiding unnecessary expenses for a week or postponing the purchase of non-essential items. Witness how this exercise strengthens your willpower and reiterates your commitment to your financial aspirations.

As you venture toward financial success, you'll encounter obstacles along the way. Life's unpredictable, throwing unexpected expenses, market downturns, and personal setbacks our way. Yet, resilience acts as the impenetrable armor that shields your willpower during these trying times. Embrace challenges as opportunities for growth and learning, and you'll emerge stronger and more resolute in your financial pursuit.

Remember, willpower, discipline, and resilience aren't inborn traits; they're skills to be honed and nurtured. By consistently practicing self-discipline, managing the allure of instant gratification, and cultivating resilience, you create a formidable trio that will steer you toward financial abundance.

Building wealth is not a quick sprint; it's an enduring marathon. Just like in any marathon, there will be hurdles to overcome. However, armed with the right mindset and tools - willpower, discipline, and resilience - you can surmount these challenges and unlock the door to a financially secure and fulfilling life where your dreams become your reality.

In our fast-paced world, instant gratification is everywhere, constantly enticing us to spend our hard-earned money on fleeting pleasures. However, a key attribute of successful wealth builders is their ability to practice delayed gratification.

The decision to forgo that expensive vacation or the latest gadget might seem challenging in the short term, but it pales in comparison to the rewards that await those who prioritize long-term financial goals. Sure, that new gadget might be calling your name, and that flashy vacation could be oh-so-tempting. But remember, every choice has a price, and by choosing patience, you're unlocking a treasure trove of future wealth. So, hold steady, stay true to your purpose, and see the price tag of that shiny advertisement as an opportunity to rest on your laurels in your future retirement golden empire instead. Remember, it's not about sacrificing your happiness, but rather, it's about optimizing the balance between present joys and future prosperity that aligns with what you truly desire.

While short-term gains may tempt us with their allure, true prosperity lies in the mastery of long-term planning and a mindset that embraces the infinite horizon of wealth. In a world of instantaneous gratification, it is vital to understand that wealth is not instant; it is an everlasting skill to build upon. The journey to financial success requires patience, persistence, and an unwavering commitment to your long-term goals.

If there is one magic ingredient in the recipe for long-term wealth, it is the accumulative power of compound growth. Like a snowball rolling down a snowy hill, your wealth can exponentially grow over time. Understanding the magic behind compound interest is the foundation of intelligent financial planning.

Without a clear sense of purpose, your financial journey will drift aimlessly. Imagine a ship setting sail without a destination in mind – it meanders in the sea, following every gust of wind. To chart your course, define your dreams and aspirations, and align them with your financial goals. Your vision should be audacious yet deeply meaningful, inspiring you to stay the course and motivating you to navigate through turbulent waters.

In the digital age, we have grown accustomed to instant results, but in the world of wealth, patience is the ultimate virtue. The allure of rapid gains might tempt you to venture into speculative endeavors, but true wealth is built on a bedrock of steadfastness. The road to abundance is paved with consistent efforts, wise decisions, and the art of delayed gratification.

The marathon of prosperity is not without its challenges and setbacks. During your financial voyage, you may encounter rough waters and unanticipated obstacles. Embrace these moments as valuable lessons and opportunities for growth. Reflect on your decisions, analyze your choices, and adjust your strategy accordingly. The ability to learn from failures is the foundation of resilience.

As you navigate the wealth path, resist the allure of short-term gains and remain steadfast in your commitment to long-term planning. Harness the power of compound growth and watch as your wealth multiplies over time. Stay true to your vision, adapt to challenges, and cultivate the patience needed to achieve lasting success. The path to prosperity lies in understanding that wealth is not a fleeting destination but an eternal journey. Embrace your financial voyage to be one of purpose, stability, and everlasting abundance.

Time, the most valuable currency in existence, governs our lives. Unlike money, fame, or power, time cannot be bought, sold, or regained. It flows steadily, never pausing or rewinding for anyone. Each of us is granted a finite amount of time, and how we choose to utilize it determines the path we tread on the road to wealth.

Time is a great equalizer; we all have the same 24 hours in a day. The distinction between those who amass wealth and those who struggle often lies in how they manage their time. Time management is the art of aligning daily actions with overarching long-term financial goals. It's all about those small, consistent actions taken daily that create an avalanche of achievement.

To unleash the true potential of time, one must identify clear, purposeful financial objectives and break them down into actionable steps. Like a master architect constructing a magnificent building, you must meticulously plan and execute your financial blueprint. Small, consistent steps, taken daily, yield remarkable results over time. Use the advantage of time now because the best way to have time on our side is to start today! Invest in up-leveling your skillset so that in 1-2 years, you can raise your rates and rise above the competition. Invest in your stock portfolio for compound interest to compound in 5-10 years. The sooner you start, the more time your money has to grow. By investing today, you're setting the stage for a financially free future. Invest in learning and reading so that even in one year, you'll be smarter and make better decisions each year toward increasing your wealth.

Imagine if you dedicated just one hour a day to learning something new. That's 365 hours in a year! In two years, you'll have amassed 730 hours of knowledge. With this newfound expertise, you can raise your rates, gain respect in your industry, and leave your competition eating your dust. Whether it's learning a new language, mastering software, or honing your negotiation skills, every minute you invest in yourself today is a minute that will pay off exponentially tomorrow. Imagine you wake up one year from today, and everything has changed. Your bank account is healthier, your skill set is sharper, and your confidence is off the charts. How did this happen, you ask? It happened because today—right this very second—you decided to take action and seize the advantage of time. The secret to transforming your life lies in starting where you are with what you have right now.

Imagine time as a river that carries us through life. We can either float lazily downstream, letting it carry us wherever it pleases, or we can paddle with purpose, navigating towards our financial dreams. Just as a skilled sailor harnesses the wind to navigate the seas, successful wealthbuilders understand that time must be harnessed and utilized wisely.

Time and money are inseparable partners in the quest for wealth building. One of the most potent concepts in finance is compound interest. Compound interest is not just a mathematical formula; it is the very essence of how time multiplies wealth. Imagine you toss a tiny pebble into a calm pond, and what happens? Ripples! Those little ripples grow and collide, creating waves that can move mountains. That's compound interest! Start early, and your money will churn and grow like a financial whirlpool, bringing in all those sweet returns. It's a wealth-building cyclone, and you've got the power to set it in motion. Don't wait for some time; get in the compound interest game and claim your treasures!

Harnessing the power of time through early investments, delayed gratification, and purposeful time management is the key to unlocking your financial dreams. Make each moment count, and let time propel you toward a life of abundance and financial freedom. As you set sail on the boundless seas of opportunity, carry with you the realization that time is not just a limited resource but the most potent asset you possess on your path to prosperity.

15

Reframing Wealth

We need to break away from the notion that wealth is inherently corrupt or immoral. Instead, let us consider wealth as a tool—a resource that can provide opportunities, safety, comfort, and positive impact. It is not wealth that determines moral value but how it is earned and utilized. Wealthy individual can use their resources to create opportunities, not only for themselves but for others as well, and can contribute significantly to social development and progress. Wealth can be a powerful tool to facilitate expansion, innovation, and positive social change.

Wealth, when combined with a conscientious moral compass and integrity, fosters an environment where creativity, growth, and good work ethics can be rewarded. It allows individuals the freedom to explore their potential, nurture their talents, and ultimately contribute to the betterment of society.

Furthermore, wealth provides an avenue for increased autonomy. Wealthy individuals have the privilege of choosing the life they want to lead. They can make decisions that cater to their interests and passions without being constrained by the relentless necessity of survival. Wealth can afford one the luxury of time to explore and contribute to society.

Poverty, on the other hand, is often romanticized as a form of virtue, a path towards humility, and detachment from materialistic desires. However, such narratives do not impart the hardships and limitations that come with poverty.

Poverty often brings about a lack of access to education, healthcare, and other basic necessities of life, making it a significant barrier to personal development and societal contribution. It cultivates an environment of scarcity, where the primary concern is survival, not self-actualization or the advancement of society. Virtues often associated with poverty—simplicity, humility, and virtue—can be practiced irrespective of one's financial standing. Hence, it is not poverty that should be lauded as virtuous, but people can cultivate these qualities separately from money.

The discourse around wealth and poverty must avoid extreme views and moral absolutism. Wealth is not synonymous with greed, nor is poverty with virtue and vice versa. They are simply different economic conditions that people find themselves in, and their moral ethics depend on the individual's character and behaviors that are unrelated to one's financial net worth.

An equitable society would strive not to romanticize poverty as noble but to eliminate it. A pragmatic approach to wealth doesn't mean the relentless pursuit of riches at any cost but rather viewing wealth as a tool for personal growth and societal enhancement. It's about understanding the power that wealth holds and the potential for good that can be achieved when it's utilized ethically and responsibly.

It's important to remember that the aim should be to create an environment where wealth is accessible to all who are willing to work for it— an environment where poverty is not a permanent, inescapable trap but a temporary condition that can be overcome through opportunity, hard work, and societal support. Wealth, when understood and harnessed in this light, can indeed be ethical.

16

Wealth and Society

Firstly, let's dissect the most profound aspect of wealth: its capacity to empower. Economic resources provide individuals and societies with the tools to manifest their destinies. Wealth allows for self-expansion, offering a buffer against societal and environmental shocks. It provides a highway upon which we can design and live our desired lives.

Wealth is the driving force behind most technological advances and social innovations. It bankrolls the creation and dissemination of life-saving medications, funds the exploration of uncharted frontiers in space, and invests in sustainable energy solutions to tackle climate change. To put it succinctly, without wealth, our global society would stagnate, left to wither on the vine of its unfulfilled potential.

Society is not a static entity but an evolving organism. This evolution is driven by the continual human pursuit of a better life—more comfort, more knowledge, more opportunities, more growth, and more evolution. In this constant quest, wealth serves as the lifeblood that nourishes societal progress.

Wealth Fuels Innovation and Progress

Innovation, the creative engine that drives societal advancement, often requires substantial investment. This is true for all sectors, from technology and medicine to education and the arts. Without wealth, these sectors could not conduct the necessary research, develop new ideas, or implement advancements, thereby stagnating our societal advancement. Wealth, thus, is the oil that keeps the gears of innovation turning.

Wealth Enables Education and Skill Development

Wealth facilitates education and skill development, allowing individuals to reach their full potential and contribute meaningfully to society. Without wealth, many would be deprived of the opportunity to learn, grow, and realize their dreams. The absence of advanced intelligence would inevitably lead to societal stagnation.

Wealth Fosters Trade and Global Connection

Wealth drives trade, allowing countries to exchange goods, services, and ideas. This not only stimulates economic growth but also fosters global connections, cultural exchange, and mutual understanding. Without wealth, countries would retreat into isolation, and the rich tapestry of our interconnected world would revert to limitation.

Wealth Builds Infrastructure

Wealth is necessary for building infrastructure — roads, schools, hospitals, libraries — the backbone of our society. Without adequate infrastructure, society cannot function efficiently, and progress becomes a restricted possibility.

The list can go on forever! Having expounded on the critical role of wealth in societal progress, we need to ponder: what happens if wealth ceases to flow? As hinted earlier, a lack of wealth could lead to limitation and societal stagnation, causing our civilization to languish and be deprived of the essential nourishment it needs to evolve.

Imagine a tree, its branches stretching towards the sky leaves rustling in the sunlight — a symbol of growth and life. Now imagine the water that nourishes it suddenly drying up. The tree's growth halts; it wilts, its leaves shrivel, and slowly, it withers away and then sets off a chain reaction that affects the entire ecosystem. Similarly, without the nourishing flow of wealth, on the individual level as well as in our society, it would stagnate and wither away, a shadow of what it could have become as a flourishing and advancing society.

This exploration into the value of wealth sheds light on its integral role in our society. Without wealth, we risk stagnation, denying ourselves and future generations the progress and advancement of human evolution. Hence, as we move forward, let us not dismiss the significance of wealth but instead strive to generate and distribute it wisely, keeping the vision of a prosperous future for future generations.

Moreover, wealth aids in the cultivation and preservation of culture and art. Private patrons have historically financed artists and thinkers, giving birth to eras of creativity like the Renaissance. Modern philanthropists also support museums, orchestras, and libraries, making culture accessible to all. Wealth, in this sense, is not just an economic asset; it is the lifeblood of cultural vitality and diversity.

However, it is essential to differentiate between wealth as a tool and the intention behind its usage. Wealth is a force multiplier. It amplifies the underlying character and intent of its possessor. When coupled with benevolence and foresight, it can uplift societies and spawn monumental achievements. But when paired with greed and short-sightedness, it can lead to exploitation and deprivation.

Therefore, the dialogue around wealth shouldn't be a binary of good versus evil. Instead, we need to shift our focus to its equitable distribution and ethical usage. Possessing wealth isn't a problem in itself; it becomes problematic when it is hoarded, used for destructive purposes, or acquired through unjust practices.

We must also remember that the concept of wealth extends beyond monetary richness. It includes an abundance of knowledge, emotional intelligence, relationships, health, and time, among other things. The pursuit of wealth should be balanced with the cultivation of these other, less tangible forms of riches.

In the grand scheme of things, wealth isn't inherently good or evil. It is a societal tool, and like any tool, its moral value is determined by its application. This realization invites us to think about wealth differently - not as an end, but as a means to create a more prosperous, equitable, and enlightened world.

Therefore, let us not demonize wealth but strive to understand it better, distribute it more fairly, and use it more wisely. Let us harness the power of wealth to do good and, in doing so, elevate not just ourselves but our entire global community. To each of us lies the potential to utilize wealth - in all its forms - as a vehicle for lasting, positive change.

However, wealth, while necessary, is not sufficient on its own. Its distribution and use must be equitable and ethical, aimed at fostering collective prosperity rather than individual aggrandizement. It should be used to reduce inequality. Yes, self-love requires filling your cup first, but once you reach overflow, it is your chance to be a giver. The role of wealth, therefore, is not only to ensure progress but also to ensure that this progress is inclusive and sustainable. This requires faith and belief in a limitless, infinite, and abundant Universe with limitless resources accessible to everyone.

In the pursuit of spiritual prosperity and abundance, it is crucial to understand that an infinite reservoir of wealth exists in the universe, waiting to be harnessed. Limitless riches lie hidden within the cosmos in the Universe, yet to be brought to light. However, even more importantly, we must recognize that the universe itself possesses an inexhaustible source of abundance.

The very essence of our connection with the divine is intertwined with the idea that the Universe desires for us to prosper. Our creator yearns for us to lead fulfilled lives; as it expresses itself through us, it enables us to become better instruments for divine expression. By having abundant resources, we can elevate our ability to contribute positively to the world around us to serve a higher purpose.

The concept of the Universe's desire for our prosperity is often misunderstood. It is not about greed or selfishness but about living in alignment with the Universe's destiny and acknowledging that we are part of a greater cosmic plan. When we prosper, we create the opportunity to embody the divine's attributes, such as love, compassion, generosity, peace, and benevolence. It is in the act of creation and contribution that we find fulfillment and harmony with the divine. Wanting to thrive and live abundantly doesn't make you a greedy monster. It makes you a magnificent conduit for the universe's energy. When you're living in the flow of abundance, you're in sync with the cosmic flow's divine plan. You become this glorious channel for divine love, peace, and generosity. Your cup overflows, and you can pour that love out into the world, making it a better place for everyone around you.

When we have unrestricted command over the means of life, we can lead lives that reflect abundance in all aspects. This does not imply a reckless pursuit of wealth or hoarding resources; instead, it emphasizes our ability to live authentically, free from the burden of scarcity and fears. We can express our unique gifts, talents, and creativity without limitations, making a profound impact on the world around us.

To unlock this infinite reservoir of wealth, we must shift our focus away from the visible supply of the physical world. The limitations and scarcities we perceive in the material realm are transient and often products of our society's conditioning. Instead, we must train our minds to perceive the limitless riches of the infinite universe.

Let go of the fear of lack and scarcity, for they only serve to block the flow of abundance. Embrace a mindset of abundance, recognizing that every moment is pregnant with potential opportunities and blessings. Be open to receiving the gifts the universe has in store for you, knowing that there is no end to the abundance that can flow into your life.

Meditation and visualization can be powerful tools to align ourselves with the infinite reservoir of wealth. Take time each day to meditate on abundance and envision your life overflowing with prosperity. See yourself using this wealth not only for your benefit but also for the greater good, making a positive impact on the world.

As you cultivate a deep sense of gratitude for the abundance already present in your life, you will attract even more blessings. Gratitude is a magnetic force that draws more to be grateful for, allowing you to appreciate the richness of life in all areas.

Remember, you are a co-creator with the divine, and your destiny is intertwined with the limitless abundance of the universe. Embrace your divine birthright to live a life of abundance. By recognizing the hidden gold within you and the vast riches of the universe, you will embark on a transformative journey of money mastery that will enrich not only your life but also the lives around you.

17

Wealth Expands Life

Wealth can be the universal key that unlocks doors and pathways that would otherwise remain unattainable to those without it. Education, healthcare, opportunities for self-expression—all these are largely accessible through wealth. Wealth can function as a catalyst, enabling access to quality education, broadening horizons, offering opportunities for personal and professional growth, and affording a sense of security that encourages the exploration of one's potential.

Before delving into the heart of the matter, it's crucial to appreciate the many dimensions of wealth. Wealth is not solely about financial affluence but other dimensions of life—health, intellectual, emotional, social, professional, and more—that expand our horizons and enable us to lead enriched lives in all dimensions. Wealth, in this sense, is the fuel that powers the engine of self-actualization and pushes us to reach our zenith of potential in all areas of our lives.

When we view wealth through this broader lens, we start to recognize its crucial role in fostering our freedom and self-expression. Money, knowledge, emotional intelligence, and connections – these are tools that allow us to transform our raw potential into realized greatness and to cultivate and express our individuality. They grant us the freedom to explore, take risks, fail, learn, and grow our minds, body, and soul. With these resources, we are more able to escape the stifling grip of mere survival, more able to tune in to the rhythm of our divine purpose and follow our true heart's desires. This freedom becomes a potent force that propels us toward our life's destiny. It liberates us from the limitations and constraints that ordinarily stifle human potential. No longer confined to a treadmill of survival mode, we are free to explore the pinnacle of our highest potential.

However, it is equally important to remember that the absence of wealth – or rather, the scarcity of these resources – can hamper our growth and restrict our freedom. When we are caught in the daily struggle to survive, the luxury of self-exploration and self-expression often feels limited. Our minds become preoccupied with fulfilling basic needs, and our spirits are hemmed in by the pressing realities of want and scarcity. The story of our lives becomes more about survival than about living out our wildest dreams.

Wealth, in all its forms, serves as a powerful tool for self-expression, exploration, and expansion. Without it, our lives may become primarily focused on fears, making the journey to self-actualization arduous. It's in balancing wealth with navigating our lives as our true, authentic selves that we can reach our highest potential and live our best lives. Wealth allows for freedom, adventure, risk, self-exploration, and more opportunities toward achieving self-actualization. Wealth creates space for unlocking your highest potential and living a life of purpose and fulfillment. Wealth allows the continual process of expansion, self-discovery, and self-progress.

At its core, self-actualization is the process of becoming the best version of yourself, living a life that aligns with your deepest values, passions, and aspirations. Imagine yourself as a seed planted in the soil of possibilities, gradually breaking through the surface, reaching for the sun's warmth, and blossoming into a magnificent tree. Self-actualization is that journey of growth and unfolding, where you transcend the limitations you once thought defined you.

In the modern world, it's easy to get lost in the noise of societal pressures. Many of us wear masks to fit in, afraid to reveal our authentic selves. But the path to self-actualization begins with embracing who you truly are, with all your quirks, vulnerabilities, and uniqueness. Screw trying to fit into society's cookie-cutter mold! You're not meant to be a cardboard cutout; you're meant to shine like a supernova you were born to be. Embrace your quirks, your messy bits, and your shining brilliance – that's what sets you apart from the mundane crowd. Authenticity empowers you to break free from the chains of conformity, empowering you to love and accept yourself for who you truly are.

You possess a treasure trove of talents, strengths, and passions waiting to be expressed and nurtured. Take a moment to reflect on your passions and what brings you joy. Identifying your strengths empowers you to channel your energy into activities that resonate with your essence, propelling you toward self-actualization. Embrace your strengths with enthusiasm, and know that they are meant to be showcased to the world.

To embark on this life-changing journey, you must be willing to venture within, confronting both your light and shadow. Carve out time for introspection – a quiet sanctuary where you can unravel the layers of your being. Journaling, meditation, or simply being in nature can serve as portals to your inner self. Self-actualization requires some serious soul-searching. Let go of distractions and dive deep into the abyss of your emotions, dreams, and solitude. It's time to go within because that's where metamorphosis begins.

As you awaken to your true potential, set goals that are truly mean-ingful to you. Ask yourself, "What do I want to accomplish in this lifetime?" Your goals should align with your core values, passions, and purpose. When you are driven by authentic goals, obstacles become stepping stones, and setbacks become opportunities to learn and evolve to achieve new heights. Set goals that make your heart pound with excitement. No more lukewarm dreams – go for the ones that light your soul on fire!

Self-actualization is the path to expansion and becoming your highest self. Embrace challenges as valuable lessons rather than roadblocks. Each obstacle presents an opportunity to rise stronger, wiser, and more confident. Cultivate a growth mindset, viewing every experience as a stepping stone toward your higher self. At the root of self-actualization is the principle of 'growth.' Growth is not a passive, automatic process; it is a deliberate and continuous journey that requires active participation. In this context, wealth serves as a supporter, providing the necessary support for personal growth and evolution. It finances education, unlocks doors to professional training, funds entrepreneurial ventures, and underwrites the leisure required to meditate, contemplate, and pursue intellectual and emotional development.

No matter who you are—a physician, a teacher, or even a salesman—you have the power to transform your life and attract all the abundance you desire. You hold the key to your future. Once you reach closer to self-actualization, your heart will grow like one of the Universe to change lives and the world for expansion. Your greatness and service will attract abundance like a magnet.

Reaching self-actualization changes your energy field by expanding it, where it vibrates at the frequency of peace, freedom, and joy. Imagine all the people living authentically to their truest selves and highest potential. They become the ultimate healers, saving lives left and right with unshakable inner power by simply spreading light, kindness, and joy. Patients won't be able to resist the magnetic force of this healing light, like moths to a flame. Think about speakers spreading the word of abundance and changing lives. People crave authenticity, and they'll flock to someone who embodies truth. Preach the truth, and they'll be drawn like a magnet.

These principles apply to everyone. With your authentic service that makes an impact on someone's life, the universe will reciprocate your service with you through monetary value or other means of value. Opportunities will present themselves, and your alignment to truth, faith, and purpose will make you keenly aware of them. Be proactive in seizing these opportunities, for each step towards progress will lead to more exceptional opportunities. No more settling for mediocrity —embrace your potential and envision your greatness; no matter how challenging your situation may seem, you've got the power to change your story.

Gratitude is the catalyst that propels you toward self-actualization. As you progress on this journey, take time to appreciate every milestone, every lesson, and every moment that shapes you. Gratitude fuels positivity, attracting more abundance into your life and opening doors to new opportunities. Remember, there is no lack of opportunities in the cosmos for those who provide impactful, great service. The universe is designed to respond to your energy. It will reflect your state of being at all times. Are you carrying a grateful heart? Are you in alignment with your truth?

Wealth enables us to rise above the fundamental concerns of survival, which all too often consume our thoughts and energy. By relieving us from incessant worries about meeting basic needs, it allows us to indulge in introspection, discover our strengths, explore our passions, and understand the role we wish to play in the grand tapestry of life. Only when we're free from the cycle of survival can we aspire to reach the pinnacle of our highest self and manifest our highest potential – the state of self-actualization and enlightenment.

However, it's essential to comprehend that wealth doesn't guarantee self-actualization; it merely provides the resources. The journey to self-actualization remains a deeply personal endeavor unique to each individual. It requires self-awareness, persistence, and a deep sense of purpose. Wealth allows for freedom and resources, removing the tangible obstacles that might stand in the way. Ultimately, the journey to self-actualization must be walked by the individual.

Consider wealth as an empowering resource that can be used to broaden horizons. A financially secure individual can afford to travel and experience diverse cultures, expanding their worldview and perspective. They can invest in innovative ideas and start businesses that not only create employment but can also revolutionize society. They can fund philanthropic projects, effecting positive change in communities and indirectly improving their sense of self-fulfillment and purpose.

While wealth may appear superficially as a status symbol, its real power lies in its ability to grant freedom—freedom to spend time as you wish, explore your interests, deepen your knowledge, contribute to society, and, more importantly, shape the trajectory of people's lives with your impact. Money, in this sense, is not just currency. It's a transformative force, a conduit to opportunities that allow us to expand, realize our truest selves, and ultimately evolve human consciousness on a grand scale.

The paradox of wealth lies in its neutrality. It doesn't inherently signify success or failure, virtue or vice, fulfillment or emptiness. Its true value lies in how it's used. When seen as a means rather than an end, wealth can be a mighty instrument for self-actualization, societal change, and, ultimately, collective human expansion.

So, as we accumulate wealth, let us see beyond its superficial implications. Instead, recognize it as a tool to further human potential, both within ourselves and for society on a grander scale. Wealth is not merely about the power of buying but the power of being, service, and expanding life. It's a vehicle for personal evolution, a catalyst that pushes us to reach the pinnacle of our highest potential, and a resource that, when used wisely, can assist in the pursuit of transforming lives. Real wealth lies not in your bank account but in the person you become in your quest to attain your highest self for abundance.

18

Money Blocks

I n our universe, abundance is as natural as the sun's warmth and the wind's caress. It flows around us and within us, humming with a richness that is our birthright, our inheritance as beings endowed with the spark of consciousness. Yet for many, this bounty remains a mirage, an unreachable oasis just over the next dune of life's desert. Our efforts to achieve it can often feel like trying to capture the ocean in a net. What is this elusive barrier that keeps us away from the ocean of abundance? It's an emotion as old as humankind itself: fear. It's the barrier that blocks the path of abundance, preventing it from flowing freely into our lives.

Fear is the greatest thief of abundance because it stifles our creative energies, curtails our dreams, and reduces our willingness to take risks. It manipulates us into settling for less than what we deserve. Fear tells us that abundance is a scarce commodity, available only to the chosen few. But this is an invalid misconception. Abundance is our birthright. It is as infinite as the universe itself. Recognize fear as a falsehood, an illusion that has no power over you unless you allow it.

Fear is a masterful thief. It prowls in the shadows of our consciousness, making us doubt our worthiness and question our potential. Fear whispers that we aren't deserving, that abundance is for others but not for us, and that it separates us from what is rightfully ours. Fear is the greatest liar with the most deceitful mask.

When fear holds the reins, we can't reach out freely to grasp the opportunities that life presents us. We hesitate, we question, and we overanalyze. The abundance that could be ours remains just a thread away, a thread we are too fearful to grasp. Fear, after all, is the phantom architect of the 'scarcity mindset,' the belief that there isn't enough to go around, that we must cling to what little we have. It makes us myopic, forcing us to view the world through a pinhole instead of the vast, panoramic perspective of possibility.

Abundance is more than just material wealth. It's a mindset, a perspective, a philosophy of life. It's about recognizing the world as a place of infinite potential, filled with opportunities and adventures waiting to unfold. But to perceive the world this way, we must first confront and disarm the fear that clouds our vision.

Fear is an illusion and exists only in our minds. Yet, its grip can be so strong that it keeps us from chasing our dreams, from opening our hearts, from embracing the very abundance we yearn for. Fear shackles us in a prison of 'what ifs' and 'if only,' trapping us in the past we can't change and a future we can't predict. Fear is a magnifying glass to fixate on the negative, to take a cynical view of our capabilities and circumstances. Fear distorts reality, painting a grim picture where our mistakes are monumental and our successes are mere footnotes. It's like a distorted mirror, reflecting an exaggerated, grotesque version of ourselves, undermining our faith in our abilities and overshadowing our accomplishments. Remember that fear magnifies the negatives only when we let it. By shifting our focus, we can also magnify our victories, no matter how small. Each triumph, each leap forward, is a testament to our resilience, a tribute to our spirit. Let's amplify these notes in our life experiences.

We must recognize fear for what it is—a natural human response, a protective instinct. But we must also understand that fear is not always right. Our lives are not solely a series of risks to be mitigated but also opportunities to be manifested. Yes, there are moments in our lives when the glass is half-empty, but life is also half-full. We can choose to focus on the full half, the side brimming with potential and promise.

There are good and useful fears, such as protecting you from danger. Some fears can be negative, such as emotions like guilt, shame, and resentment, which lower your wealth consciousness. They trap you in a cycle of negativity that makes it difficult to see and seize opportunities for financial abundance. Guilt, shame, and resentment are a trio that thrives on low vibes, keeping you stuck in the financial mud and oblivious to the golden opportunities that surround you. These emotions are like grouchy old trolls under the bridge to wealth, and they've got a way of linking arms and singing fear anthems that keep us stuck in Scarce City instead of skipping off to Abundanceville.

Guilt often arises from the feeling that we have done something wrong, whether it's failing at a business venture or making a poor financial decision. This guilt breeds self-doubt, undermining our confidence in making future financial decisions and, thus, lowering our wealth consciousness. Doubt is fear's accomplice in crime, a sinister voice whispering that we aren't enough. It suggests that we don't possess the skills, talents, or intelligence to attract abundance into our lives. This, too, is an illusion. You are enough. You were born enough. Doubt erodes self-esteem, causing us to believe that we are undeserving of abundance. Combat doubt by fostering self-love and self-belief. Remember, you are the universe in ecstatic motion.

Shame, on the other hand, is a deep-seated feeling of inadequacy, often a result of societal expectations or personal comparisons. If we see others amassing wealth more rapidly, it can trigger feelings of shame about our financial status. This sense of shame creates a mental block, holding us back from recognizing and seizing opportunities for financial growth. Resentment often stems from feeling unfairly treated or believing that others have opportunities we don't. This emotion blinds us to the opportunities around us, filling our minds to focus on negative thoughts and limiting our potential for financial prosperity.

Another barrier of fear is the illusion of unworthiness. Many of us, through life's trials and tribulations, have adopted a belief system that tells us we are undeserving of abundance. This is perhaps the most destructive of all illusions because it makes us actively reject abundance when it tries to flow into our lives. Always remember that your worthiness is a given, not something you have to earn. You deserve abundance simply because you exist.

Overcoming fear isn't about banishing it from our lives. It's about acknowledging its existence, then deciding not to let it take over, and learning to manage it healthy. It's about understanding that fear is a warning, not a command. Appreciate fear for what it's good at—when there's a bear or something. Otherwise, calm down fear and say, "I got this one, thanks."

When you feel fear, take a moment to recognize it. Acknowledge it. Say, 'I see you, fear. I feel you. But I will not let you overcome me or dictate me.' Then, move your decisions towards your dreams. Every step you take despite your fear is a step closer to abundance.

Understanding these barriers is the first step. However, the path to removing them demands courage, introspection, and patience. It requires us to question and redefine our beliefs about ourselves and the world around us. It involves nurturing a mindset that sees opportunities instead of obstacles and chooses love over fear in every situation.

Start today by challenging your fears, doubting your doubts, and affirming your worthiness. Embrace the fact that you are an integral part of this infinite universe. Just like the stars, the moon, and the sun, you, too, are made of stardust and meant to shine your light. Only then will the wall of illusion start to crumble, allowing the river of abundance to flow freely into your life.

Recognize and Acknowledge: The first step to overcoming any fear is to recognize its existence and understand its source. Recognize when feelings of guilt, shame, or resentment are creeping in, and acknowledge them for what they are - temporary, transient emotions, not defining characteristics.

Practice Self-Forgiveness: We all make mistakes. It's an integral part of our learning and growth. Instead of wallowing in guilt over past financial mistakes, forgive yourself. Use these experiences not as weapons for self-flagellation but as tools for learning and improving.

Reframe Your Narrative: Instead of associating shame with your financial situation, reframe your narrative. Understand that everyone's financial journey is unique and influenced by different factors. Embrace your journey, with all its ups and downs, and use it as a stepping stone towards financial abundance.

Cultivate Gratitude and Abundance Mindset: Resentment thrives on a scarcity mindset. By cultivating an abundance mindset, you focus on the plentiful opportunities around you. Practice gratitude for what you already have and see how it opens your mind to future possibilities.

Seek Professional Help if Necessary: Lastly, don't shy away from seeking professional help. Therapists and financial advisors can provide guidance and tools to navigate your emotional landscape and make strategic financial decisions.

The walls that block the flow of abundance in our lives are not there by chance. They are not punishments, nor are they permanent fixtures. They are simply reflections of our internal beliefs and fears. But the good news is that just as we have the power to build these walls, we also possess the power to break them down. Don't let fear be the dictator of your financial destiny. Confront these fears, learn from them, and ultimately, turn them into your stepping stones toward financial prosperity.

Remember, the world is abundant with opportunities, but our fear makes them seem scarce. It's a grand illusion that fear portrays. In our journey for abundance, it's essential to understand that it doesn't only relate to material wealth. Abundance, in its true form, encapsulates love, joy, creativity, health, emotional and spiritual richness. These are the treasures we seek when we talk about living an abundant life.

The key to unlocking abundance is faith in our abundant Universe and clearing the illusions of fear. When fear is cast aside, the world is your oyster, heaped high with opportunities, experiences, and wealth beyond measure.

In this journey, you may falter. You may stumble. You may even fall. But remember, each fall is an opportunity to rise higher. Each stumble is a lesson to learn from. And each falter is a moment to pivot.

By understanding fear and learning to navigate through it, we unleash the power to tap into life's abundance. We open the doors to possibility, we invite opportunity, and we welcome the richness that life offers. This is the path of abundance. This is the path we are meant to tread.

Hold the hand of your fear. Look it in the eyes and remind it who's in control—your higher self, guided by the Source, the Universe. Abundance is available for you. All you need to do is step beyond your fear and claim it.

In the end, confronting fears is about understanding their role and using them as a catalyst for growth. It's about realizing that life is full of limitless potential and possibilities. It's about choosing not to be imprisoned by the glass of half-empty fears but emancipated by the half-full possibilities. This perception shift—this embrace for a fuller, richer life—truly embodies the potential for a life beyond your wildest dreams.

Affirmation:

"I am more than my immediate circumstances. I am capable of building wealth and forging my own prosperous path by co-creating with the loving Universe for an abundant life beyond my wildest dreams."

19

Heal Your Money

You're not here to scrape by, pinch pennies, or live a life of just instant noodles. You're here to metamorphose into the abundant warrior within you and reach your highest potential. It's time to switch from a scarcity mindset to one of abundance. Remember: you're not just pursuing wealth; you're transforming to your higher self through expansion along your divine journey. It's about welcoming money into your life, not just as a necessity but as a tool for expansion.

Let's start this journey by acknowledging the scarcity mindset that may be currently holding you captive. It is an all-too-common trap: the belief that there isn't enough—not enough time, resources, or money. This limiting belief stems from fear—fear of lack, loss, never having enough, etc. But remember: fear limits the mind and blocks the flow of creative opportunities. It paralyzes us and keeps us stagnant.

For far too long, many of us have been trapped in an abusive relationship with our 'broke selves.' We are constantly reminded of our limitations, our scarcity, and the things we cannot afford. Our mind replays this narrative of hardship and deprivation over and over until it has become the only story we know. We view ourselves through the lens of lack, always needing more, never satisfied, and ever-distant from the abundance we desire.

Yes, it's time to break up with your 'broke self,' but more than that, it's time to heal and redefine your relationship with wealth. Stepping out of this fear and breaking free from the scarcity mindset requires a shift. A transformative, everlasting shift. Breaking up with your 'broke self' is just the beginning. The beginning of a new relationship with money, a relationship built on appreciation, love, and abundance. A relationship where you are the master, where you wield the power, and where you create wealth. This is the power of wealth consciousness. It's time to step into it.

The first step is to learn to forgive yourself for past financial mistakes. They were lessons, not life sentences. Let go of guilt, resentment, and shame, as these emotions only serve to lower your wealth consciousness. Embrace the lessons learned, make peace with your past, and move forward with renewed hope and newfound wisdom.

We are all shaped by our experiences, the lessons we have learned, the trials we have faced, and the triumphs we have celebrated. Yet, too often, we bear the weight of past financial mistakes like an unwelcome ghost, a heavy burden that hinders our progress rather than propelling us forward. It's a common narrative: you are not alone, and you always have the power of choice to change your story at any point in time.

So, you've messed up. Maybe you started a business that crashed and burned. Or perhaps you bet on a 'sure-thing' investment that turned out to be a hoax. You might have even squandered your cash on impulsive spending sprees from a mental breakdown. And now, you're doing the Financial Walk of Shame, weighing you down by guilt, resentment, and a bank account that's gasping for air. But hey, aren't we all human?

You may view these experiences with regret, guilt, and shame, but instead of dwelling on the past, you can choose to learn from it, to find the rainbow in the aftermath of a financial storm. What if you chose to believe that these were life lessons, not life sentences?

Shift your perspective. Replace regret and resentment with gratitude and forgiveness. Be grateful for the lessons these financial missteps have taught you that you could have never learned otherwise. They have, after all, made you wiser and stronger. Accept that these experiences were part of your journey, part of your growth, and necessary lessons you would've never learned otherwise. Remember, the Universe is on your side, and everything is for your growth.

Financial mistakes, while painful at the moment, can be invaluable lessons. They show us where we've gone wrong, offer a mirror to our consciousness, and provide us with greater wisdom to navigate the future. We have to become aware first and decide to change. The key to turning these setbacks into stepping stones lies in forgiveness.

Start by forgiving yourself. Acknowledge that you made the best decisions you could with the information you had at the time. Recognize that everyone makes mistakes, and what defines us is not the blunders we've made but how we rise from them.

Forgiveness is not about erasing the past but about making peace with it. Letting go of guilt does not mean ignoring the consequences of your actions, but instead acknowledging them, learning from them, and using them as stepping stones for greater understanding, wisdom, and better decisions.

Remember, emotions like guilt, shame, and resentment only serve to lower your energetic frequency and wealth consciousness. They trap you in a cycle of negativity that makes it difficult to see and seize opportunities for financial abundance. By releasing these emotions, you clear the path to elevate your wealth consciousness and welcome more opportunities into your life. Forgiveness is like sage to clearing your energy field for peace. So, break free from the chains of past financial mistakes. Let go of guilt, embrace the lessons, make peace with your past, and stride into the future with renewed hope, wisdom, and the will to succeed. After all, you are not the product of your past; you are the architect of your future.

Embrace the truth that your financial past does not dictate your financial future. Your mistakes do not define you, but how you respond to them does. With forgiveness, acceptance, and future-focused action, you can transform your financial regrets into financial resilience. Just narrow your focus on the future. Use the past lessons learned to chart a better course. Armed with your newfound wisdom, commit to better financial decisions, prudent planning, and savvy investments. Forget the past to be any different because the future is unwritten, so write to your wildest imagination about what could be possible.

The next step to reclaiming power over your money begins with understanding wealth consciousness. You are not what you earn, you are not your occupation, you are not your debts or your savings. You are an abundant spiritual being with a soul and spirit connected to the infinite, vast Universe, and the power to create wealth resides within you.

The abundant self is not afraid of money, nor is it controlled by it. It doesn't operate from fear or scarcity. Instead, it operates from a place of abundance, a place where you understand that money is not your master; instead, you are the master of money and your life. This shift in perspective to becoming a master of your money transforms not only your relationship with money but also your entire life.

Abundance is believing in the limitless and infinite Universe. It's a shift from a fear-based mentality to one of love, gratitude, and faith in a higher power. When you truly trust in the infinite universe, in its bounty and generosity, you will start attracting the very things you desire. Money is energy. Like everything else in the universe, it is attracted to those who welcome it with love and gratitude. Embrace the abundance within you as you are part of this infinite Universe. This is not about wishful thinking but about acknowledging your innate potential and the miracle of your life. The scarcity mindset is a trap to keep you powerless, but you can break free from it. The universe is infinitely abundant, and so are you, as you are part of the universe itself.

Reclaiming your power over money is not an overnight process but a journey of self-discovery and transformation. It's a journey where you learn to understand the true nature of wealth, change the way you think and feel about money, and embrace the abundance that is waiting to flow into your life.

Begin to see yourself as a money magnet. See yourself as a person of infinite potential, with the ability to attract and generate wealth in all its forms. When you embrace this abundance mindset, you'll find that money will be attracted to you. It's drawn to those who believe in their worth and potential with light.

The foundation of wealth consciousness is paved with gratitude. The practice of gratitude has the incredible power to shift your mindset from scarcity to abundance. Every day, no matter your financial situation, find something to be grateful for. Even the smallest thing can shift your perspective and make you realize the abundance you already possess.

But remember, this isn't just about getting rich. The journey of the abundant warrior is one of transformation. As you shed your scarcity mindset and welcome abundance, you will also acquire wisdom and transformation. It's the process of who you are becoming as you journey through this mission in your life.

Wealth is about your ability to experience life to its fullest. It's about the love, joy, and light that you can derive and share with others. Wealth consciousness is about believing in the limitless Universe and its infinite possibilities. You have to feel worthy enough to strive to be your highest version of yourself, that you deserve the best life has to offer, and actively work towards manifesting it. Your wealth can fund your dreams, create opportunities for others, and bring positive change to the world. As you become more, you can do more. That is the ultimate expansion. That's the power of the warrior spirit within you.

20

Money is Energy

Our Universe is a grand orchestra of energies, both seen and unseen, known and unknown, all of which interact and weave together to form the physical and metaphysical world we experience. Within this framework, money is not merely a piece of paper or a digital number on your bank statement. It is an energetic entity that becomes a mirror of your energetic resonance. For some of you, this whole concept may be causing your eyebrows to meet your hairline.

Everything in the Universe, from the galaxies swirling in the heavens to the thoughts and emotions that surge within us, vibrates at specific frequencies. These frequencies act as a unique signature, an energetic thumbprint that shapes our interactions with the world. Our experiences, including our financial ones, are dictated by these frequencies. When you view money as an energy form, you understand that it, too, carries its own frequency.

Money's frequency, however, is neutral. It doesn't intrinsically possess qualities of 'good' or 'bad,' 'right' or 'wrong.' Instead, it responds to the frequency we project. Your perception and attitude towards money create the tone of your interaction with it. If your internal narrative is one of scarcity, fear, or unworthiness, you may find that your external financial reality mirrors those feelings. Conversely, if your mindset shifts towards abundance, value, and deservingness, money can respond in kind.

The secret of attracting money is not about wishing harder, grinding your teeth as you work 100-hour weeks, or clutching onto every penny in fear of running out. It lies in adjusting our energetic vibration to align with the vibration of abundance. We must shift our understanding of money as being hoarded to seeing it as a flow of energy that is always available, always flowing, and circulating.

Energetic resonance with money is not a one-time action but a continuous process. It involves assessing and reassessing our beliefs, feelings, and attitudes toward money and making conscious decisions to shift our perceptions from fear to love, from lack to abundance, and from scarcity to prosperity.

Understanding that money is a form of energy and comes from the Universe is not a path to instantaneous wealth. Instead, it is a journey of self-awareness and personal expansion. The Universe offers an infinite reservoir of energy, and by aligning our energetic vibrations with it, we can tap into this endless source. This alignment does not mean just financial wealth but a richness of experience, relationships, joy, and everything life has to offer.

The energy of abundance is akin to the deep resonance you feel when your heart is brimming with joy or the exhilarating rush of freedom when you're bound only by the horizons of your imagination, or the profound experience of love that allows you to embrace everything as it is and everyone as they are.

So, how do we tune into the frequency of abundance, and how does it correspond with joy, freedom, and love? Imagine a radio. This simple device receives an array of frequencies, each representing a different station and world of sound. Your life is similar. You can tune into the frequency of scarcity, fear, and lack, or you can choose to resonate with the frequency of abundance, joy, and love of the highest vibrations.

Abundance is an omnipresent frequency. It's the sun that warms our planet, the air that fills our lungs, the grains of sand that cover our beaches. When we connect deeply with the natural world, we are reminded that we are part of an infinite cycle of giving and receiving, life and death, love and freedom. We are all part of this rhythm, this energy of life's existence. We only disconnect from this frequency of abundance when we forget our worth, lose our faith, or disconnect from our authentic selves and the world.

The key to rediscovering abundance lies in the feelings of joy, freedom, peace, and love. These emotions aren't just feelings; they are energetic vibrations and frequencies and your tuning forks to abundance. Use your emotional state and intuition to know your feelings as a barometer to measure your energetic frequency. How you feel will reveal the energy you express. When you feel joy, you will emit joy. When you feel abundance, you will emit abundance. The Universe will deliver accordingly to match the address of the energetic frequency you emit to the field of the Universe.

Joy is the music that makes your soul want to expand. When you feel joy, you're saying a resounding "yes" to life. You're opening the door to receiving and stepping into a flow of abundance that's ready to flow to you. Joy amplifies the frequency of abundance. It's not contingent upon what you have but how you perceive and engage with the world.

Freedom is the infinite space in which you can explore, express, and experience the totality of your being. Freedom allows you to be your authentic self. When you are free, you are open to the flow of abundance.

Love is the most potent frequency, the universal language that permeates everything. Love transcends boundaries, dissolves fear, and embraces all of life. In the act of giving and receiving love, abundance manifests most beautifully.

When you resonate with the frequency of joy, freedom, peace, and love, you align yourself with the vibration of abundance. This isn't about doing or striving but about being present and connecting to the Source/Universe. You'll be flowing in alignment with what the Universe offers to your doorstep. It's about allowing, accepting, and embracing life in all its beautiful complexity. By living in the energy of joy, freedom, peace, and love, you are not only tuning into the frequency of abundance but also becoming the frequency of abundance.

21

Detox

Toxic energy, whether negative energy or toxic individuals, obstructs our flow, drains our positive energy, and pulls us away from our higher self, which has the power to create and manifest abundance and happiness. The reason is simple: negativity consumes space that can otherwise be filled with opportunities for expansion and abundance.

Think of your energy field as a garden. Just like a gardener wouldn't want weeds to strangle the growth of their precious plants, you wouldn't want toxic energy and people to stifle your growth. When we allow toxic energy to seep into our lives, it drains our resources and diverts our attention from what truly matters to us, keeping us from manifesting our goals, dreams, and desires.

In our journeys, many of us inadvertently become repositories of others' negative energy, thinking we must help or save people around us where we get sucked into their drama and absorbed into their negative energy field, leaving us feeling drained and powerless. This often results in our energy field becoming cluttered and static, which ends up lowering our vibrational frequency and energy, holding us back from our highest potential. It leaves us feeling stagnant, reverting us back to our past selves, such as relapsing to our old subconscious behaviors of self-sabotage, procrastination, laziness, etc.

The first step to reclaiming your power and enhancing your potential for prosperity is to recognize the sources of toxic energy in your life. This requires a deep and honest introspection to identify patterns, relationships, and habits that might be draining you. Remember, awareness is half the battle won.

Toxic energy can be equated to an emotional or psychological pollutant. It's a pervasive, negative force that can drain your energy, cloud your judgment, stifle your growth and happiness, and impact your overall mental health. People who consistently emit this energy are often referred to as 'toxic people.' Their negativity is contagious, leaving you feeling emotionally exhausted, stressed, or demotivated. Recognizing toxic energy is the first significant step to eliminating it from your life. But how do you identify it?

1. Consistent Negativity: Observe if your interactions with an individual often leave you feeling drained, overwhelmed, or overly negative. Toxic people are experts at spreading pessimism, blaming others, and rarely taking responsibility for their actions. They are consistent downers and fault-finding machines.

2. Emotional Manipulation: Toxic people are adept at emotional manipulation. They use guilt trips, gaslighting, or playing the victim card to shift blame or control you. They are pros at yanking your emotional strings.

3. Lack of Respect for Boundaries: They tend to disregard personal boundaries, whether emotionally, physically, or personally. You might find them prying into your private matters, dictating your decisions, or bombarding you with messages without respecting your personal space and time. Your "No Trespassing" signs are invisible to them. They will gleefully poke their noses into your personal space, physically, emotionally, and psychically.

4. Frequent Criticism: Constructive criticism is essential for personal growth. However, toxic individuals often resort to unnecessary criticism or belittling remarks, leaving you feeling inferior or incompetent.

5. Unreciprocated Efforts: Relationships are built on mutual respect and reciprocity. If you find yourself constantly giving and receiving nothing in return, or if the relationship feels one-sided, it might be time to reassess.

Eliminating Toxic Energy

Identifying toxic energy is one thing; dealing with it is another. Once identified, it's crucial to eradicate this negative influence from your life. Muster the courage to sever ties with toxicity. This could mean setting firm boundaries with negative individuals, distancing yourself from environments that don't serve your highest good or journey, and breaking free from self-defeating habits. It might feel challenging initially, but remember that every time you say 'no' to what doesn't serve you, you're saying 'yes' to your path to abundance.

1. Set Boundaries: Establish clear boundaries and stick to them. Whether it's setting a do-not-disturb time or refusing to entertain negative discussions, let your preferences be known.

2. Practice Self-care: Your emotional health should be your priority. Regularly practice mindfulness, meditation, or any activity that uplifts your mood and rejuvenates you.

3. Communicate: Address the issue. Convey your feelings without blaming or attacking. Use 'I' statements to express how certain behaviors impact you.

4. Seek Professional Help: If dealing with toxic energy that is affecting your mental health, seek professional help such as therapy, etc.

5. Limit or Cut Off Contact: If all else fails, it's okay to limit or completely cut off contact with toxic people. Your well-being and peace should always be your top priority.

Remember, eliminating toxic energy and people from your life is not an overnight process. It requires examination and patience. Never compromise on your mental health, and remember, it's okay to choose your peace over pleasing others.

If your life were a fabulous, shiny Lamborghini, toxic energy is the gunk in the fuel tank. It's an insidious downer that drains your joy, dulls your sparkle, and leaves you feeling about as energetic as a sloth post-Thanksgiving dinner. People soaking in this energy are champions of doom and gloom, capable of turning a sunny day into an apocalypse. And they've got an uncanny knack for making you feel as shrunken as a deflated balloon.

We've all experienced those energy-sucking, soul-draining folks who seem to believe the world thrives on a never-ending stream of chaos and drama. They're like a live TV news channel spreading bad news like a toxic energy swamp; it's grimy, messy, sticky & icky.

Not everyone is purely virtuous or entirely evil; most people exist on a spectrum of humanity that spans from our best selves to our worst. This dichotomy isn't limited to the external world but also resides within the intricacies of our personalities. As human beings, we harbor both toxic and healthy traits. The key lies in our willingness to acknowledge and do the self-work to work on our harmful patterns and behaviors, understanding their impact on others. The path to self-awareness and personal improvement is challenging, demanding a conscious effort to examine our habits and adjust our actions. Choosing to respond thoughtfully rather than react impulsively and opting for kindness moves us closer to the healthier side of our higher selves.

In our quest for self-betterment, it's vital to practice compassion towards ourselves and others. Everyone is navigating life with the emotional tools at their disposal. Everyone is doing the best they can with the tools they have in their emotional toolkit. Some of these tools may be rusty, some might be blunt, and some might not be right for the task at hand. Some of us have a Swiss Army knife of emotional skills; others are trying to navigate life with a rusty old spoon. These tools vary greatly; some are underdeveloped or unsuitable, while others may be more sophisticated. The variance in emotional skill sets should be considered, especially when interacting with those who appear more deeply rooted in their negativity. Many are grappling with personal traumas and fears, often unconsciously reliving past experiences and traumas—a phenomenon akin to a never-ending, repetitive cycle known as "Repetition Compulsion." Repetition compulsion is a psychological phenomenon in which an individual repeatedly enacts or re-enacts certain behaviors, scenarios, or traumatic events, often unconsciously. They might be unknowingly following scripts shaped by past experiences, continually echoing trauma and fear. Sigmund Freud, the great explorer of the human mind, first shone a light on this shadowy director. He observed how we, the puppets of our past, are drawn into repeating our history as if compelled by some unseen force.

Consider the individual who, having suffered neglect in childhood, finds themselves magnetically drawn to aloof partners. Each relation-ship, a mirror of the past, reflects the familiar sting of neglect. Or witness the executive who, despite their brilliance, repeatedly sabotages their success at the pinnacle of achievement. These are not choices made in the full light of consciousness but replays to a tune played by personal history and embedded in the subconscious mind.

Remember, the subconscious mind fears the unknown and finds safety in the familiar. Someone might be stuck in their trauma because they don't know any better, and safety might feel uncomfortable because it is unfamiliar to the subconscious mind. This is the paradox at the heart of repetition compulsion: we are drawn, time and again, to situations that may bring us pain or sorrow simply because they resonate with the comfort and familiarity of our past.

Our behaviors are not entirely our own making; they are also the products of conditioning. Throughout our lives, we are trained by our experiences. When a pattern of behavior is reinforced, whether positively or negatively, it becomes etched into our psyche, creating a path of least resistance that we are inclined to follow blindly and repeatedly.

The compulsion to repeat is not merely a trap; it is also a quest for mastery. The individual may unconsciously seek to recreate the situation or emotions associated with the trauma in an attempt to resolve or better understand it. Each repetition is an unconscious attempt to gain control over the uncontrollable, to rewrite the script of our past traumas with a different ending. It is a misguided attempt by our psyche to heal itself.

If one is stuck in the repetition compulsion of their trauma, it can be a significant hindrance, trapping individuals in a cycle of fear and preventing them from living in the present. It can lead to a repetitive narrative where one is constantly reliving past thoughts, emotions, and experiences. This cycle robs one of the opportunity to harness the magic of the present and its potential opportunities. For some, this means being stuck in a continuous loop of their past, replaying the same emotions and patterns daily. In this state, people can become trapped in grim storylines, repeatedly manifesting a reality based on fear-based old narratives. Consciously working to manage one's emotions and heal from trauma is crucial to breaking free from this cycle and embracing the potential of the present.

To break free from the shackles of repetition compulsion, we must first recognize its existence. This demands a journey into the depths of our subconscious, a confrontation with the ghosts of our past. It is a challenging path, but it is also one of liberation. By understanding the roots of our compulsion, we can begin to untangle ourselves from its grip and reclaim our power to write our own story. By bringing it into the light of consciousness, we can break its spell and emerge with a deeper understanding of ourselves and a newfound sense of freedom.

Let's pull the brakes for a second and take a look in the rearview mirror. We've all been "that person" at one time or another, you know, the "Debbie Downer," aka the negative one. We've all had moments where we were just calling for love, feeling as prickly as a cactus but just as huggable. But those sour folks in your life who are making things miserable? They're just like we once were. They're brimming with toxicity and acting out because they're running on empty love and being disconnected from the Source/Universe.

Some people don't have the luxury of time or resources for self-reflection, personal development, or therapy. Everyone, deep down at the core of their being, desires love, peace, safety, and happiness. These are truths that link us together, irrespective of our differences. This recognition can help us foster empathy and understanding, even for the individuals we label 'toxic.' It's also essential to remember that underneath their adverse behaviors, they too are on their personal journeys, much like ourselves, and the best we can do for these toxic people in our lives is to wish a prayer of love, peace, and safety that we, ourselves, desire. We might not have the bandwidth to keep them in our lives, but we can send loving energy toward them for healing through prayer. Doing so not only liberates them but you as well. It's a simple yet potent act of kindness that can catalyze a ripple effect of positive energy, and this matters because we live in a Universe that operates on energy. In this journey from darkness to light, from toxicity to health, the most vital insight is this realization of our shared humanity. We are all united in our struggle and our aspirations. Let's try to understand this and create a world that's less judgmental and much more compassionate. By understanding this, we can create a more compassionate world for ourselves and others.

Our life is not merely about the distance we travel but the direction we choose. Let's make a conscious choice today to move towards love, peace, kindness, and compassion and, in doing so, allow others the space to do the same. So, let's be the love warriors we are and shine a light on the darkness. Let's deliver the one thing these people need more than anything: love. It's not just about healing them - it's about transforming the world with one act of love at a time.

Negative Thinking

Removing toxic energy is not merely a matter of distancing ourselves from external negativity; rather, it's a profound journey into the depths of our own being, purging the internal toxicities that afflict our spirit. This includes the negative self-talk, the pervasive cloud of pessimism, and the fear-driven narratives that often dominate our inner dialogue. These elements can be as corrosive, if not more so, than external sources. The path to cleansing involves the nurturing of our inner landscape with empowering affirmations, a profound sense of self-love, and a vocabulary that radiates positivity.

On average, a person has about 60,000 thoughts a day that are mostly negative and repeated thoughts from the day before. Beneath the veneer of our modern lives, ancient primal instincts still dictate much of our behavior and thought processes today. One of these, which can have an immense impact on our well-being, is our tendency to focus more on negative events. This hardwired predisposition is known as negativity bias. It's like an old survival tool from our evolutionary past, deeply etched into our biology, but in the contemporary world, it often seems to cause more anxiety than solutions. We still carry ancestral traumas and fears as we navigate our world today. In the distant past, our ancestors faced daily physical threats in their environments. Survival necessitated swift response to potential danger. Those who quickly perceived and reacted to threats were more likely to survive and reproduce, passing on these valuable traits to subsequent generations. This formed an evolutionary emphasis on being alert to negative events. Ignoring the sight of a juicy, ripe berry might lead to a missed meal, but overlooking the rustle of a predator in the bushes could mean the end of one's life. Those spear-toting, fur-wearing, mammoth-hunting cavemen were all about survival, and to do so, they had to pay keen attention to the threats. Miss a lovely sunset? No biggie. Miss a saber-toothed tiger? Well, next, you're tiger chow, and that's the end of your gene pool. So we're hardwired to get hung up on the negative because, once upon a time, it was a literal lifesaver.

Our brains thus evolved to react more strongly to negative stimuli. This negativity bias has been invaluable in our journey as a species. However, the problem arises when this prehistoric programming meets the social, intellectual, and emotional complexities of 21st-century modern life. Fast forward to today, and our lives are a smidgen less deadly. But our primordial instincts haven't gotten the memo. They're still stuck in survival mode, freaking out about the modern equivalent of saber-toothed tigers in today's world, interpreted from the road-raged driver to the snide comment from our boss that feels life-threatening. Our primal instincts haven't caught up with our yoga-practicing, self-help reading, soy latte-sipping selves tucked away in our cozy concrete buildings.

Today, we rarely face mortal danger in our day-to-day lives. The threats we encounter are less tangible and more psychological. Yet, our brain treats these modern concerns with the same gravity as those life-threatening scenarios our ancestors faced. Consequently, we can easily find ourselves trapped in a perpetual cycle of stress, anxiety, and fear.

Negative thinking is the mental shackles that hold us back from our true potential, hindering us from attaining the prosperity that is available to us. Negativity often lurks unseen, quietly undermining our efforts and sapping the life out of our aspirations. Negative thinking prevents wealth by focusing on fears and limitations that slowly but surely erode our conviction to pursue and attain prosperity. To understand the real effects of negative thinking, it's essential to realize that our mind is like an unfathomably fertile garden. The thoughts we plant—positive or negative—are like seeds; they eventually grow and bear fruit. Negative thoughts, when planted, grow into weeds that choke the life out of other thriving plants we have planted. They cloud our minds with fears, and before long, they can make us feel powerless.

Wealth often comes from the inside, from our ideas, service, and labor. It is a product of a mindset that encourages creativity, persistence, and growth. Negative thinking, conversely, stifles creativity, breeds fear of failure, and focuses on limitations of why it's all impossible. Fears prevent you from taking risks in business; if your thoughts are dark and stormy, you're going to run for the hills at potential opportunities. When you're in fear, you miss the spot for opportunities to grow your bank account. Negative thinking also has a way of perpetuating itself. If you believe you'll fail, you'll unconsciously sabotage your efforts, leading to failure, which in turn reinforces your negative beliefs. It becomes a self-fulfilling prophecy.

Remember, it is in our nature, and it is our natural predisposition toward having a negativity bias. However, it is about not letting it monopolize our entire lives with doom and gloom. Being aware of this negativity bias might bring some relief as to why you might be anxious, worried, or fearful at unnecessary times.

Addictions

Did you know you could be addicted to stress, like a drug? This addiction often manifests as an unending craving for drama and chaos in our lives. Meet cortisol, your body's alarm system, also popularly known as the stress hormone. When we encounter a stressful situation, our body's fight-or-flight response is activated, and cortisol is released. This helps us become more alert, focused, and prepared to face the threat at hand. When we stumble upon some sort of scare, cortisol pops into the bloodstream and gets our body ready to wrestle a bear or sprint like a roadrunner; it's our fight-or-flight response.

Alongside cortisol, our bodies also produce adrenaline during stress, preparing us for potential dangers. This adrenaline rush can feel invigorating, sometimes giving us a sense of being fully alive. It's a strong feeling that some people come to crave, associating it with thrill and excitement. Along with adrenaline, our brains release dopamine, a neurotransmitter associated with reward and pleasure. This creates a potent, albeit harmful, cocktail that can make stress addictive. Each time we engage in drama, it triggers the stress response. The ensuing adrenaline rush and dopamine release make us feel exhilarated. This exhilaration can become so intoxicating that we may start seeking out stress-inducing situations, effectively becoming addicted to drama and stress. This stress-drama feedback loop works much like any other addiction. It starts with an intense, pleasurable experience - the adrenaline high and dopamine reward. Our brain correspondingly associates this experience with the stressful situation or the drama, leading to craving and seeking those same biochemical feelings. Over time, we may find ourselves unconsciously attracted to stressful situations, drama, and conflicts, driven by the desire to experience the adrenaline-dopamine high again. This is when we have crossed the line into stress addiction, using drama as our drug of choice.

This trio of cortisol-adrenaline-dopamine lights up chemicals in our brain like a Christmas tree akin to a feeling of a rush or high. So, we get hooked. We start chasing after stress like it's the last bus of the night, craving the rush of adrenaline and dopamine. We're no longer bystanders of the drama show; we're all consumed, committed to the role of Macbeth in Shakespeare, dramatizing with madness, thanks to this biochemical cocktail in our brains.

You might be stuck in a vicious cycle of financial drama, where your story seems to be more about scarcity, stress, and perpetual chaos. What if I told you that your addiction to drama is messing up your finances?

Financial stress acts much like any other stressor. It rings the alarm bells in your body, setting off the cortisol, adrenaline, and dopamine fireworks. When you're constantly worrying about paying bills, meeting debts, or simply surviving until the next paycheck, you're effectively stuck in a chronic state of stress. And guess what? You just might be addicted to it.

The drama around money doesn't only have to involve the stress of not having enough. It can also be about a tantalizing chase. The chase of a better job, a higher income, a bigger house. Are you trying to keep up with the Joneses? Each time you reach a milestone, you set another target, perpetually keeping yourself in the cortisol-adrenaline-dopamine loop.

This constant state of drama and stress can block your path to financial abundance. You're so caught up in the whirlwind of financial chaos that you miss opportunities for growth and prosperity that might be right under your nose. You're in such a frantic state of feeling uneasy and being caught up in your money drama, which negates you from the present moment, where prosperity manifests. Being in a continuous state of stress can impact your decision-making abilities. You may make rash financial decisions or fail to plan adequately for your future, effectively sabotaging your financial stability.

There's always something to fret about, a new thing to repair, a bigger house to strive for. You've become so accustomed to this drama that you feel bored or uneasy when things are calm and stable. Your addiction to the drama surrounding money is like chaining yourself to cigarettes: a one-way ticket to a whirlpool of smoke and mirrors, where the stakes are always high, and the rewards are dangerously low. Just as lighting up another stick that promises a fleeting embrace of satisfaction, each gossip-infused headline you consume whispers sweet promises in your ear, urging you to indulge just one more time, chase that high one more instance. Just like each puff drags you further away from clean lungs and a fresh breath, each dive into the tumultuous sea of financial scandals drags you away from your true powerhouse of wealth. Your inner self knows the value of focused, purposeful work over the frenzied pitch of the rumor mill.

You see, chasing after drama is like chasing smoke rings – ephemeral, unsatisfying, and leaving you smelling less than fresh. It's an exhausting run on a hamster wheel of frenzy, where your warrior self is lost amidst the haze. Darling, it's time to quit cold turkey. It's time to ditch the dizzying highs and nauseating lows of the drama addiction, cleanse your palette, and invite in the crisp, clean air of focused ambition and authentic passion. Throw out the cigarettes, tune out the noise, and tune into the powerhouse you were born to be, ready to burn bright, not burn out. Replace the drama with your newfound journey to investing in your abundant financial future. Step into your true self, a maven not of gossip but of grounded reality, guided not by the whims of rumor but by the beacon of your own glorious potential. It's time to stub out the drama, take a deep breath, and light up the true brilliance of a life led with purpose and determination, with your eyes on the prize, not on the gossip column because you are far too fabulous to let your time and energy go up in smoke.

So, how do you hop off the financial stress express and start walking on the sober road to abundance? Begin by recognizing your addiction to financial drama. Acknowledge that you're caught up in this fear thrill-chase-stress cycle and that it's blocking you in many ways. Once you've done this, start actively working on breaking the cycle. Adopt a mindset of abundance, focusing more on the resources you have rather than what you lack. Practice mindfulness, learn to separate your self-worth from your financial worth, and work on creating a healthy relationship with money.

It's also crucial to make informed, calculated financial decisions rather than getting swayed by the thrill of the moment. Stop making impulsive purchases and exercise a 30-day no-spending month aside from your fixed expenses such as rent and groceries. Plan for your future, invest wisely, and learn to find satisfaction in stability versus chaos. By understanding the underlying patterns and taking conscious steps to change, you can break free from the chains of money dramas and open the door to abundance. Say goodbye to the stress express and hello to your prosperous, peaceful walk in the park.

Understanding that stress addiction is a biochemical loop gives us a starting point to break free from it. The first step is recognizing and solving the problem. If you find yourself constantly in the middle of disputes, perpetually overwhelmed, or feeling a strange emptiness when life is peaceful, you might be dealing with stress addiction.

Once we acknowledge this, we can employ various techniques to rewire our brains and manage stress healthily. These may include mindfulness practices, cognitive-behavioral therapy, exercise, restful sleep, and a healthy diet. Most importantly, we can start seeking reward and satisfaction from positive experiences, slowly undoing the association between pleasure and stress.

While stress is an inherent part of life, being addicted to it doesn't have to be. In understanding the underlying biochemistry, we can not only demystify the paradox of stress addiction but also empower ourselves to step out of the turbulent cycle of drama and into a life of healthier coping mechanisms that unblock our path to abundance.

22

Becoming

The path to acquiring wealth demands not just your time and energy but also a portion of your soul, forever altering you to become the highest version of yourself that is more resilient, discerning, and wise. We're talking about a journey that pulls you out of your comfort zone and pushes you to birth into a new stage of life. The metamorphosis process is like the best boot camp ever, where you emerge as the superhuman version of yourself. True wealth is not just measured in material gain but in the depth of one's soul, the strength of one's principles, and the legacy left behind.

The journey toward financial success is often paved with trials that test more than just your perseverance—they test your morality. Every obstacle, rejection, and setback is an invitation to reflect on who you are becoming with every choice you make and the compromise you make. Will you cut corners to advance, or will you uphold your values despite delays? Will you treat people as mere stepping stones, or will you lift others as you climb?

Character is not built in moments of ease but in times of adversity. The choices you make in the shadows, when no one is watching, define your moral wealth. If the pursuit of financial abundance comes at the cost of your integrity, then it is not wealth at all—it is a slow erosion of the self. This depletes your spiritual bank account, which is the invisible force of your manifesting power. The richest individuals are not those who merely possess but those who have endured and emerged with their principles intact.

As success begins to manifest, it brings its own unique trials. The weight of wealth demands responsibility. If struggle tests your character, then prosperity tests your integrity. Reflect on how you treat others when you have abundance, as well as how you behave in scarcity. Regardless of whether you are rich or poor, who are you at your core? Will wealth make you kinder, or will it harden you? Will you share, or will you hoard?

It is easy to assume that financial success will solve all your problems, but unchecked wealth can become a gilded cage. The temptation to define your worth by your net worth can lead to a hollow existence, where no amount of riches can fill the void of a lost purpose. The antidote is simple but often forgotten: connection, expansion, and gratitude.

Wealth is not the destination—it is the byproduct of the person you become. The ultimate wealth is a life rich in meaning, connection, and ethical prosperity. The true measure of success is not in the size of your fortune, but in the light, you bring to this life and the impact you leave behind.

Just as a strong muscle requires consistent training and maintenance, the development of character must continue as your wealth grows. Without intentional growth, success can stagnate, and setbacks in personal development can ripple into every aspect of life. Every new level of success comes with its own trials, testing your discipline, values, and ability to sustain both physical and moral prosperity.

Wealth is not a final destination—it is an ongoing journey that requires continuous self-reflection and evolution. The habits and mindset that led you to success must be nurtured, or they will wither. Just as an athlete who ceases to train loses strength, a wealthy individual who neglects character development becomes vulnerable to complacency, arrogance, or declination.

Personal growth is a lifetime pursuit, just like your physical health. Dedication and consistency, like exercise, means questioning your motivations, auditing your actions, and ensuring that your decisions align with your values every single day of the week. It means not allowing wealth to create a false sense of security or superiority. A person who stops growing the moment they achieve financial success is like a tree that refuses to extend its roots—it may stand tall for a time, but it becomes fragile, susceptible to the first strong storm.

With each stage of life, new challenges emerge. At first, the struggle may be to achieve financial stability. Then, it becomes about managing and growing abundance wisely. Later, it may be about legacy—what you leave behind for future generations. At every phase, temptations shift but never disappear.

Will you let comfort dull your drive? Will you allow success to breed entitlement? Will you prioritize wealth over relationships along your journey? These are the tests that arise not in scarcity but in abundance. Those who continue to develop their character remain resilient, while those who fail to advance risk watching their empire crumble.

We realize that the path to wealth requires a continual path of self-development. Failure is not an anomaly on this journey; it is a certainty because it's necessary for the path of expansion. It is through these failures that we learn the art of perseverance and remaining steadfast in the face of defeat. This phase is characterized by grit, tenacity, and solidifying our commitment to our goals. Failure is just part of the learning curve, and the only way is forward. Trust in this process of growth and develop patience as the expression of faith on your path to prosperity. It's easy to drool over the prospect of instant riches, but remember: the tallest and strongest trees take the longest to grow. You're consciously creating your dream life with every choice and action in every waking moment.

Even in wealth, adversity is inevitable. Economic downturns, personal crises, and unexpected losses serve as reminders that money alone cannot protect you from life's unpredictability. The true safeguard is your character—the resilience you've built through years of self-discipline, humility, and a willingness to keep growing.

Adversity is not a signal to retreat; it is an opportunity to reinforce your principles. Just as muscles grow stronger through resistance, character is fortified through challenge. The wealthiest individuals are not those who avoid hardship but those who embrace it as a means of refining their strength.

The pursuit of wealth is not merely about financial gain but about becoming a person who can sustain and wield their growth wisely. The most fulfilled individuals are those who view personal development as a lifelong commitment, ensuring that their growth keeps pace with their prosperity.

To remain truly wealthy, you must keep advancing. Just as a strong body requires maintenance, a strong mind, and spirit demand possibly even more attention, so keep learning, keep refining, and keep striving for wisdom alongside wealth. Only then can you ensure that success can be sustained and accumulated.

As you soldier on, you realize that wealth isn't about hoarding gold like a miser. It's about the simple things: a good laugh, a warm family dinner, and lending a helping hand. It's about appreciation, connection, and heart. That is the good life.

So, here's what it all boils down to: wealth isn't just about the figures in your bank account. It's about who you become— your true authentic higher self, a sage, a happy soul, a generous giver.

Gratitude and humility reveal to us that wealth isn't about what we have but what we give from our hearts. It isn't about the material world but about service. It's what truly matters deep in our souls. The wealth journey cultivates deep-seated gratitude for the opportunities we have been given and the lessons we have learned along our life journey. This stage of our transformation fills us with a sense of responsibility and a desire to contribute to society for the expansion of humanity.

<h1 style="text-align:center">23</h1>

<h1 style="text-align:center">The Unknown</h1>

Our natural tendency as humans is to fear the unknown, where potential opportunities are on the other side of the common known path. Humans feel safe in their comfort zone, the predictable, familiar, and the known. The unknown is the birthplace of all possibilities, the genesis of innovation, and the breeding ground for the extraordinary. It is in the realms of the unfamiliar that we discover new paths, build unprecedented relationships, and tap into reservoirs of potential within us that we never knew existed.

Fear, with its myopic vision, fails to recognize that what lies beyond the unknown may not be a pitfall but could also be a life far beyond our wildest dreams. It habitually views the unknown through a prism of threat rather than opportunity. In doing so, it deters us from embarking on novel adventures, embracing change, and, ultimately, living a life beyond our own imagination.

The unknown, a term laden with mystery and often perceived with trepidity, is a profound echo of uncertainty that reverberates through the cavernous expanse of life. The majority of us quiver at its mystery, allowing our innate fear of the unknown to tether us firmly to the shores of familiarity. But, it is important to understand that every monumental moment, every groundbreaking innovation and every transformative decision took birth in the enigmatic womb of the unknown.

Let's let Lobsters be our wise guru into the unknown; these crustacean trailblazers have a thing or two to teach us about up-leveling our lives. Just like how a lobster outgrows its shell, humans must ditch their comfort zones to evolve. For example, a plant needs to be repotted as it grows, and for humans to expand, we need to get out of our comfort zones. Getting out of our comfort zones means doing things we've never done before, such as starting a new career, trying out that new thing we've never done before, asking for that raise, etc. Just like how a lobster knows it's time to break free from its old shell, we must shed anything holding us back, such as staying stagnant in our comfort zones.

When a lobster is ready to level up, it goes through a molting phase. The lobster's body starts brewing a new, roomier shell beneath the surface. This new shell is soft and vulnerable, leaving the lobster feeling like it's walking around without armor on a battlefield. But then comes the grand finale – the lobster's epic breakthrough moment. It's not pretty, folks. The lobster has to literally crack open its old shell to free itself from its old shell. Imagine the discomfort, the pressure, the tearing away of what was once safe and familiar. Ouch, right? But hey, this pain is the price of growth. Sometimes, growth feels painful just because it's uncomfortable. This is where you develop grit and grow stronger, and you'll reap the rewards later.

Your comfort zone, yeah, they're your old shells. They served a purpose once, but now they're holding you back from upgrading your life. Just like the lobster's newfound shell is a bit tender initially, your initial steps toward change might leave you feeling vulnerable and scared. But that's where the growth happens.

As you push through discomfort and uncertainty, you forge a stronger, more resilient you. Just like that lobster's shell toughens up over time, your skills, your attitude, and your whole self strengthen as you face challenges with boldness. Remember, the lobster's struggle to emerge from its old shell isn't a setback; it's the very essence of growth.

The lobster's journey is like a mirror to your own expansion. Growth doesn't come without a bit of pain, without shedding the old to embrace the new. The lobster's molting process is where you break from the old life and create your new, abundant life. Let go of what's holding you back, dare to crack out of that comfort zone, and emerge as your upgraded version of your future best and highest self. A new life starts from your own personal growth journey.

Think of the Universe as a hardcore personal trainer, pushing you, testing you, and making you sweat until you learn whatever cosmic lesson you need to learn to get to the next level in this game of life. But also, the Universe is like a cosmic life coach. Your trials and tribulations aren't just random occurrences – they're there for a reason, with a mighty purpose and potential for more expansion in your life.

Money is also a large factor in this Earthly life. It's there to teach us valuable lessons about ourselves and the world. Behind the veil of the Universe, everything is happening for you to learn, grow, and expand to your highest potential. Embrace these challenges. The Universe wouldn't throw anything your way that you couldn't handle. You have all the power within you to overcome these challenges and get through on the other side as a warrior and a phoenix that rises from the ashes! The Universe knows you more than you know because it is a part of you, and you are also a part of it, so keep faith that everything is happening for you and your highest good!

This does not suggest that you get an easy pass and press the snooze button all day. Still, your life is entirely your responsibility. Don't just sit back and wait for everything to fall into place, considering you are the only one in control of your own life if you feel trapped and recognize that you continue to go through the same repetitive stagnant motions from day to day. It's time to face your issues head-on, starting with resurrecting that warrior who is asleep inside you. Don't simply repeat Groundhog Day by running in a hamster wheel of destructive old habits, self-sabotaging patterns, and negativity. Are you stuck in the same problematic situation for way too long?

Stop settling for what you can get; it's time to rise to your dreams that are destined for you! You are One with the Universe; what you want is what the Universe is seeking through you. The Universe is knocking at your door, asking you to co-create the life of your heart's desire! The Universe is planting seeds in you, and it's time to nurture those seeds with your unique soul's life essence! It's time to rise to your abundant life!

Close your eyes and think of an empty canvas. The initial sight of it may provoke anxiety, an overwhelming question lurking in the back of your mind, "What should I create?" But isn't that the very beauty of it? The freedom to create anything, the liberty to explore everything—the canvas is a representation of creative possibilities born from the unknown. Each brush stroke is a step into uncharted territory, an exploration of infinite possibilities. Each color we choose, each line we draw, represents our courage to move beyond the borders of our comfort zone and explore the road less traveled.

This unexplored realm is not just an abyss of uncertainties but rather fertile ground teeming with potential—a world beyond our wildest dreams. History is an illuminating testament to this truth. Was it not in the unknown that the Wright brothers sought the miracle of flight and where Thomas Edison unearthed the magic of light? Each one of them, stepping into the darkness of uncertainty, made a reality of what was once thought impossible by the masses.

The idea of embracing the unknown is not about discarding caution but rather recalibrating our perception of what lies beyond the familiar. It is about replacing fear with curiosity, doubt with faith, and limits with infinite possibilities. It's about viewing the unknown not as a terrifying abyss but as a thrilling adventure that could lead us to discoveries that transcend our current understanding, to innovations that could revolutionize our world, and to decisions that could alter the course of our lives.

The road to befriending the unknown begins with a single, brave step—a step shrouded not with fears but with anticipation of the endless possibilities that await. As we tread this path, let us embrace uncertainty and take solace in the knowledge that every step forward is a journey toward something greater.

Befriending the unknown is a courageous exploration that requires insatiable curiosity and fearlessness. But remember, it is in this process, this daring pursuit to the road less taken, that we become pioneers of innovation, explorers of existence, and architects of a future we can only dream of. As we journey into the heart of the unknown, we write not only our own story but also create our dream life aligned with the guidance of the Universe. Every step into the unknown is a step into the realm of infinite possibilities.

By entering the realm of the unknown, you co-create with the divine intelligence of the universe. So, step onto the grand stage of life and invite the unknown to flow through you. Tune into the language of the Universe via intuition and flow with its guidance through synchronicities, coincidences, serendipities, and eureka moments. Because every great discovery, every groundbreaking innovation, and every life-altering decision sprang from the womb of the unknown. And who knows, the next one could be yours.

24

Your Money Purpose

Beneath the dull drizzle of everyday life, there's a different kind of weather pattern emerging, one of possibilities, opportunities, and abundance. This weather is not dictated by the whims of the economy or the stock market; it originates from within us, from our minds, and our attitudes toward abundance.

Embrace the concept of abundance, and you'll witness the world transforming before your very eyes. An abundance mindset is about recognizing the vast field of opportunities before us, understanding that there's more than enough to go around, and knowing that your gain doesn't have to come at someone else's loss.

With an abundance mindset, obstacles become opportunities, problems morph into potential, and roadblocks turn into pathways. Financial success is no longer a far-off dream but a tangible reality. You'll find yourself unlocking opportunities you never knew existed and achieving goals that once seemed impossible.

But an abundance mindset isn't just about increasing your wealth; it's about increasing your well-being and that of those around you. This approach isn't a solitary journey but a collective rising. Abundance is not a zero-sum game; when you win, we all win. When you become wealthy, you can bring about change and uplift others, creating a ripple effect of prosperity to flourish. Poverty does not manifest more wealth but wealth can manifest more abundance for all to rise together.

Believing in abundance isn't just about financial freedom; it's about breaking free from fear, scarcity, and limitations. It's about embracing possibilities, opportunities, and expansion. It's about saying goodbye to your financially restricted self and welcoming the master of wealth within you. It's about reprogramming your mindset, from one of scarcity to one of abundance.

Your relationship with money is like any other relationship. If it's based on fear, it'll feel draining and destructive. But if it's based on love and respect, it'll be enriching and empowering. Change the role of money from the villain in your story to an angel that can guide you to create the life you desire and manifest change in the world. You can be the human angel on earth with your wealth, by having more power to impact lives and change the world for the better.

By adopting an abundance mindset, you can become the architect of your fortune. You can shape your reality, dictate your destiny, and control your financial future. You have the power to transform your life and the lives of those around you, to create a world that's not just rich in money but also rich in kindness, joy, and abundance. Dive into the deep end of abundance, and start living the life you were born to live. A life where wealth is a means to enrich, not just to accumulate. A life where you are not just surviving but thriving, not just living but flourishing.

Money in our lives is often misunderstood, with the pursuit of wealth often overshadowing the pursuit of purpose. Take the time to explore an empowering perspective on wealth, how more money can enable you to do more good, offer you more freedom, present more opportunities, and how it ultimately becomes an expression of your values, to live your best life, and to contribute to expanding others.

Let's begin by reframing our understanding of money to a lens of abundance rather than scarcity. View wealth not as a zero-sum game but as an amplifying tool. Money, in the hands of someone guided by a genuine will to effect change, can become a powerful catalyst. Money enables you to expand your scope of impact, reaching far beyond your immediate circle of influence.

Now, consider this: each dollar you possess is a ballot paper, and every transaction is your chance to vote. You vote for what you want to exist in the world, and in doing so, you shape the world to reflect your values. This is a concept known as "voting with your wallet." The clothes you choose to wear, the food you buy, and the companies you invest in, all become a reflection of your values. However, the power to cast these votes becomes magnified with increased financial resources.

The freedom and opportunities that come with wealth are not just about greater personal comfort or material possessions. They represent a chance to effectuate real change. Imagine being able to fund a promising research project, contribute to change, or support the arts in a way that aligns with your vision. These possibilities for making a positive impact become increasingly accessible as your wealth grows.

However, as we discuss the opportunity to do good, it's crucial to remember the inherent complexities. The world's problems cannot be solved with money alone. A nuanced understanding of the complexities of social, economic, and environmental issues is vital. Money is only a part of the solution – the rest lies in our ability to leverage our knowledge, relationships, and creativity.

This balance between the power of wealth and the understanding of its limitations cultivates what we call 'conscious wealth.' It is the recognition that wealth is not about hoarding but about flowing – flowing towards initiatives and ideas that resonate with our deepest values and aspirations for a better world.

In this journey of wealth creation and stewardship, be guided by your purpose. Define the change you want to see in the world and orient your wealth towards those ends. Alongside financial plans, create impactful goals. Decide on the causes you are passionate about, and the legacy you want to leave. View wealth as a tool to accomplish these goals rather than as a goal itself.

The Potential of Money: An Instrument for Change

The power of money to create change is undeniable. With it, we can fund research, support charities, build infrastructure, and foster growth and development. Money, when used intentionally and responsibly, can become a powerful instrument for change, capable of transforming lives and societies.

It's important to remember that using money for good isn't limited to grand gestures of philanthropy. Small, everyday decisions about how we spend our money can collectively lead to significant societal change. Supporting ethically-produced products, buying from local businesses, or donating to grassroots organizations – these are all ways we can use money as a positive force.

Money: A Vessel for Spreading Compassion and Love

Our understanding of money shapes our relationship with it. If we see it as a tool for power, control, or status, it will be reflected in our actions. But when we start seeing it as a vessel to spread compassion and love, our relationship with money transforms.

To view money as a means of spreading love and compassion is to see every financial transaction as an opportunity to positively impact others. It means making choices that don't merely serve our individual needs, but that contribute to the well-being of our community and our world.

Recalibrating Your Relationship with Money

The journey to recalibrating our relationship with money starts with self-awareness. Reflect on your current beliefs and attitudes about money. Are they serving you, or are they causing stress and anxiety? How are your spending habits reflecting your values and intentions?

From there, it's about setting a new course. Embrace the neutrality of money and acknowledge your power to direct its flow. Infuse your financial decisions with intentionality, love, and compassion. See every dollar as an opportunity to make a difference, foster change, and spread goodwill.

The essence of money is defined by its user, not the currency itself. Money is neutral, and its potential is shaped by our intentions. By understanding this, we open up a new world of possibilities, where money becomes not just a means of survival, but a tool for creating a more compassionate and loving world. The power of money, when harnessed with wisdom and a generous spirit, has the potential to create a ripple effect of positive change. It offers us the freedom to act, the opportunity to scale our impact, and the platform to express our values more widely. So, remember, you're not just accumulating wealth; you're building a powerful tool to serve the world and make a change. Let your money become a force for good, a vote for a better world, and a testament to your purpose.

25

Giving is a Sign of Abundance

There is a profound connection between generosity and prosperity, revealing the transformative power of adopting a giving mindset on the journey to achieving true wealth. Imagine a lush garden bursting with vibrant flowers and bountiful fruits. Just as a garden flourishes through nurturing care, so too does prosperity blossom through acts of giving. When we give freely, we sow the seeds of abundance in our lives and the lives of others. Generosity cultivates a cycle of positivity, creating an environment where opportunities and blessings multiply.

The universe operates on the principle of reciprocity – what you give, you shall receive. When you give generously, whether it be your time, knowledge, or resources, you send out a powerful message to the cosmos. The universe responds in kind, opening doors and presenting opportunities that align with your giving energy and intentions. Embrace this law, and you will find that as you enrich the lives of others, your own life will be enriched beyond measure.

Meaningful wealth encompasses meaningful connections with others. By being a giver, you create a deep connection with the world around you. The relationships you forge through acts of kindness and generosity become pillars of support on your journey to success. People remember and appreciate those who give genuinely without expecting anything in return, and these connections can be invaluable in both personal and professional spheres.

A giver embraces the concept of abundance, knowing that there is more than enough to go around. This mindset is a stark departure from the scarcity mentality that often plagues our current society today. When you view the world through a lens of abundance, you attract prosperity, as you no longer operate from a place of fear but from a place of love, possibility, and expansion.

The giver's ripple effect is akin to the butterfly effect—an idea from chaos theory suggesting that a small change in one part of a system can have far-reaching consequences in another. Your act of giving, no matter how seemingly insignificant, has the potential to change the trajectory of someone's life. Consider a young student who receives a scholarship due to your contribution. That student, now with access to higher education, may even go on to create groundbreaking innovations or cure cancer. Your generosity catalyzed this transformation, and the effects continue to spread, creating a lasting legacy that transcends generations.

The beauty of being a giver lies in the feedback loop it creates within ourselves and the world. As we give, we inspire others to give. Witnessing the transformative power of our actions motivates us to do more, fueling a cycle of compassion and kindness throughout society.

Beyond individual actions, this ripple effect can extend to organizations and societies. When businesses prioritize social responsibility and give back to their communities, they foster a culture of empathy, enhancing employee morale and customer loyalty. In turn, these employees and customers are more likely to engage in their acts of giving, amplifying the impact even further.

The act of giving taps into an abundant reservoir of resources—

love, kindness, and compassion—that only grows with each act of true generosity. As we give, we learn to appreciate the intangible wealth we possess, and our perception of abundance shifts. Furthermore, the universe has a way of reciprocating our generosity. When we give without expectations, life has a way of giving back to us in unexpected ways. Opportunities, connections, and experiences unfold, enriching our journey beyond measure.

Embracing the giver's mindset is not just about doing good; it is a profound path to personal character and positive transformation. As you embark on this journey of giving, remember that every act, no matter how small, sends out ripples of love and compassion. Trust in the profound impact you can have on people and the world, and recognize that your actions impact others.

While riches amassed in a lifetime may dwindle, the impact of a giver's legacy endures through generations. Think of the great philanthropists who have left indelible marks on the world by dedicating their wealth to worthy causes. Giving allows you to create a legacy that extends far beyond your lifetime, a legacy of positive change that shapes the world for the better.

Above all, being a giver enriches your own life with a sense of fulfillment and happiness that transcends material possessions. The joy derived from helping others and making a difference in their lives is a reward that money cannot buy. This happiness creates a positive feedback loop, spurring you to achieve greater heights in both your personal and financial pursuits.

In the pursuit of prosperity, we must redefine our understanding of wealth. It is not merely the accumulation of riches but the cultivation of abundance in all aspects of life. The act of giving is a beacon of light that guides us on a path of purpose and significance, and through it, we discover that true wealth lies not only in what we have but in what we can give to others. So, embrace the spirit of generosity, and you shall find that by giving, your spirit uplifts with richness and fulfillment.

26

Alignment

In the vast tapestry of life, each of us is born with a unique thread woven intricately into the fabric of the universe. This thread is our true self – the essence of who we uniquely are, and it holds the key to a life of true abundance and fulfillment. It is time to unlock the secrets of authenticity, accept and love ourselves wholly, and venture on a journey that aligns us with our soul's purpose.

Embracing our authentic selves begins with a profound understanding that we are not accidents in this cosmic universe. The universe specifically chose each one of us, endowing us with distinctive gifts and talents waiting to be shared with the world. This realization is empowering and liberating, for it means that we are not meant to settle for lackluster lives. We are destined to live our dreams and co-create our lives with the divine Universe.

The path to everlasting abundance lies in authenticity to who we uniquely are. When we choose to embrace our unique souls, we unleash a torrent of inner power, joy, and freedom. We become in sync with the universe's rhythm, like a river flowing effortlessly to the sea. This alignment is the key to unlocking the abundance that life holds for us, a bounty that goes beyond the material world.

But how do we begin this transformative journey? It starts with self-acceptance, accepting that, as humans, we all have our own flaws and imperfections. They are a part of you, but they do not define you. The beauty of authenticity lies in acknowledging both the light and the shadow within us and still choosing to love ourselves unconditionally. Let go of the shackles of comparison and societal expectations. Embrace your uniqueness and let it shine bright, guiding others to do the same. Authenticity is majestic, and when you show up as your true self, you permit others to do so, too.

Discovering your life's purpose is a beautiful quest, and often, it is closely intertwined with doing what you love. Look deep within your heart, for there lies the answer to what sets your soul on fire. What brings you joy when time seems to stand still? Follow that passion, no matter how small it may seem, for it is the key to unlocking your purpose.

The journey to authenticity and true abundance may not be without challenges, but it is undoubtedly the path worth taking. When you live in alignment with your soul's callings, the Universe conspires to support you. It opens doors, sends opportunities, and connects you with kindred spirits who are meant for you.

In moments of doubt, remember that the Universe specifically chose you to be born for this. Your unique thread is woven into the grand tapestry of life for a reason. By being authentically you, you contribute to the symphony of existence, making it richer, more vibrant, and more beautiful.

So, dear soul, embrace your authentic self fearlessly. Live the life you were born to live, and in doing so, watch as true abundance unfurls before you like a blooming flower. The joy, peace, and positive energy that radiate from your authentic core will attract miracles and blessings beyond measure.

Trust in the journey, for it is one of self-discovery, expansion, and unending love. Remember that living authentically is not just about attracting abundance; it is about becoming a conduit for goodness, compassion, and transformation. By being true to yourself, you become a beacon of light that inspires others to shine their own unique brilliance.

Once you unite with your authentic self, you will open a clear channel to your intuition connected to the Source/Universe to guide you on your highest path. Intuition, that little whisper from your inner compass, transcends logic and reasoning. It's the gut feeling, the soft voice nudging you in the right direction. To step into this realm, we need to silence the noise of our monkey minds and create a sacred space for introspection. Practices like meditation, journaling, and mindfulness are your trusty companions on this manifesting journey. They're your tickets to forming a profound connection with your intuition and spotting the subtle signs and synchronicities that point the way to your purposeful life.

Once your intuition is awakened, you waltz into the world of inspired action. This isn't about hustling or pushing yourself; it's about flowing and letting your intuition take the lead. Manifesting abundance is a profound inner shift—a beautiful harmony between your desires and connecting to the wisdom harbored in the divine cosmic Universe.

We've been conditioned to believe that financial prosperity is solely the result of relentless work. However, lurking within us is a hidden treasure trove—a reservoir of untapped potential that defies logical boundaries. This treasure trove is your intuition—a whisper from your inner guide that transcends mere intellect. It's the deep knowing, the gut feeling, guiding you toward a path bathed in abundance through inspired action.

But how do we tap into this wellspring of wisdom? The journey commences with silencing the clamor of your thoughts, creating a sacred haven for introspection through meditation. Meditation paves the path to a profound connection with your intuition. As you do so, you become attuned to the subtle cues and synchronicities that weave through your life—these are the breadcrumbs leading you to the realm of your true divine purpose.

Once your intuition is awakened, it's time to embark on the next step of inspired action—an elegant alignment with your inner wisdom and authentic desires. This isn't about forcing or controlling; it's about letting your intuition be led via inspiration. Manifesting wealth isn't a mere endeavor of the mind; it's a deep transformation where your desires and the wisdom of your intuition converge harmoniously. You'll embark on a quest to rewrite the narrative of your limiting beliefs, setting off on a journey of personal transformation where intuition becomes your guiding light. This journey isn't for the timid—it's an exploration of the depths of your being where you'll align with your higher self and summon abundance with authenticity.

Embrace your authenticity, live your purpose, and watch as the Universe unfolds your path. This is your time, and you are ready. Your abundant, purposeful, and authentic life awaits – go forth and make it a masterpiece!

The Universe

As we delve deeper into the mystical nature of the universe, we begin to understand it as vibrant energy and unity consciousness woven together by the threads of each individual's soul and imprint of energy. Our thoughts are intricately connected to cosmic energy, and by harmonizing with its higher intelligence, we unlock the power to manifest our deepest desires.

At the heart of this transformation lies the realization that we are not isolated beings in a chaotic universe but part of a grand consciousness. Each thought, emotion, and intention we emit sends ripples through the fabric of reality, resonating with the energies that flow through the cosmos. The universe listens, responds, and conspires to bring forth the essence of our focus. We are the co-creators of our reality, shaping our destinies through the force of our minds.

To tap into this cosmic intelligence, we must shift away from the mindset of rivalry and embrace the boundless potential of creativity. When we compete with others, we create barriers that hinder the flow of energy. However, when we collaborate and appreciate the uniqueness of every individual, we unlock a vast reservoir of creative power that transcends the boundaries of limitation. We're not here to battle it out in some cage match. Oh no, we're here to embrace collaboration for limitless possibilities. When we ditch the comparison game and start appreciating the genius in ourselves and others, the whole universe teams up to support our collective collaboration. We become the epic co-creators of our reality, manifesting our energies and intentions into our reality.

Gratitude emerges as a vital key to unlocking the doors to the divine infinite Universe. As we cultivate a genuine appreciation for the abundance that surrounds us, we open ourselves to the influx of peace and love that emanates from the cosmic divine heart. This unification with the universe's frequencies allows us to access infinite resources and blessings that were previously out of our energy field. Gratitude expands our awareness, making us conscious of the interconnectedness of all things and the limitless possibilities all around.

Through consistent visualization, unwavering faith, and profound gratitude, we launch our intentions into the divine manifestation. The universe responds to the energy behind our desires and intentions, shaping reality to bring our dreams into manifestation. The act of setting intentions and flowing with the Universe becomes an act of surrender, releasing our aspirations into the formless energy that binds all of creation. Our clear intentions get catapulted into the cosmos, and the universe starts orchestrating events that come in the form of coincidences, synchronicities, and signs from the universe to manifest our dreams. This is where we tune into our intuition and work with the natural flow of things, not against it, and that's when the real magic starts unfolding. So, when you feel it's right through feelings and intuition, it syncs with and aligns with the high vibrational energy of the Universe with feelings of love, peace, light, gratitude, and joy.

Creative energy is the driving force behind this journey of manifestation. It is the spark that ignites our dreams and propels them forward. By aligning ourselves with the rhythm of the Divine Universe and working within the established pathways of nature and society, we enter a harmonious flow that guides us toward the realization of our visions. This doesn't imply that we shy away from ambition or effort but rather that we embrace our unique roles by co-creating and manifesting with the Universe and acting in concert with the grand design.

This journey to abundance is an active engagement with the universe, where we consciously direct our mental attention and take meaningful steps each day. As we move forward, we contribute value to every exchange, creating a ripple effect that amplifies growth and prosperity for all those involved. Our unshakeable faith, clear vision, unwavering purpose, integrity, service, and gratitude infuse our endeavors with positive, energetic vibrations, magnetizing success and wealth toward us.

In this grand consciousness, we become the instruments through which the universe expresses its infinite creativity. As we attune ourselves to the cosmic Universe in harmony with the flow of existence, we unlock the power to create the life our hearts desire. With every thought, we compose our reality, and with every intention, we add another note to the cosmic score. Align your energy to feel good with the Universe and embark on a journey of co-creation with the profound force that permeates all of existence.

<h1 style="text-align:center">27</h1>

<h1 style="text-align:center">Manifesting</h1>

Your life force energy is the energy that animates your being, directs your destiny, and is central to your prosperity. Understanding and harnessing this life force energy is vital for those who yearn to invite abundance into their lives. Many people search for these externally, often overlooking the abundant source of power that resides within themselves. The key to opening up this treasure trove of potential lies in strengthening your life force energy and directing it toward the things you desire.

Begin by visualizing your life force as a river. This river starts as a small trickle but can grow into a powerful waterfall, carving paths through mountains, bringing life to deserts, and feeding the vast, endless ocean. This river of energy is ever-present within you, coursing through your veins, and your task is to channel it, increase its flow, and direct it consciously towards attracting positivity and abundance.

The first step is cultivating self-awareness. You must understand your thoughts, feelings, and beliefs about wealth and prosperity. Often, negative perceptions and fears about money inhibit the free flow of our zestful life force energy. By challenging these fears, one can start to unlock their full potential. Practicing mindfulness and meditation can help you observe your thought patterns, identify these blockages, and slowly chip away at them.

In order to manifest abundance, the first step is to examine the beliefs you hold about money. These beliefs are often deep-seated, imbued in you by your upbringing, societal norms, and personal experiences. They act as filters through which you perceive your financial realities. Consider a common belief: "Money is the root of all evil." With such a notion deeply ingrained, the subconscious mind, which does not discriminate between positive and negative, may work to keep you away from money, interpreting this belief as a protective measure. However, replace this belief with "Money is a tool that can be used for good," and the outlook shifts dramatically. Money no longer becomes a symbol of moral degradation but a catalyst for positive change. Then, you will feel good about money and associate positive feelings towards money, resulting in welcoming and receiving money with ease.

Belief, though powerful, is just the foundation. It needs to be amplified by imagination and emotion. Just as a plant requires sunlight to grow, your belief in wealth manifestation needs the warm rays of vivid imagination and passionate emotions. When you imagine your desired financial reality—whether it's earning a certain amount of money, owning a home, or running a successful business—you plant the seed for this reality in the fertile soil of your subconscious mind. Emotional investment in this imagined reality then serves as the water that nurtures the seed, allowing it to sprout and grow. However, belief and imagination are not a magic pill that instantly manifests wealth; they merely set the stage for necessary actions. Believing that you are wealthy can inspire creative solutions, spark inspiration, and enable persistence in the face of obstacles, all of which are crucial for financial success.

Your beliefs are a powerful starting point. Without these empowering beliefs about being worthy of receiving abundance, capable of becoming rich, and deserving of wealth, money energetically blocks from entering your field. Your positive belief is what allows money to be welcomed into your home and energetically attracts it like a magnet.

When it comes to money, the words and beliefs you hold act as a self-fulfilling prophecy. How you speak about money is the way money will respond to you. To harness the power of language in manifesting abundance, we must first delve into the realm of your money language.

Your life, in many ways, is like a mirror that reflects the language you use. Your words aren't just words. They're like magic spells, conjuring up your reality and shaping your world, especially when it comes to money. If your money dialogue is all about scarcity and lack, you're casting a "broke" spell on yourself. But if you can tap into the power of the right words for abundance, you can transform your cash flow from a mere trickle to a majestic waterfall.

If you've ever caught yourself uttering phrases like "I'm broke," "I can't afford that," or "Money doesn't grow on trees," you've unconsciously set a financial script for the life of your money to play out. These sentences cast an underlying spell for your reality that money is scarce, hard to obtain, or perhaps not destined for your possession. This negative dialogue influences your actions, decision-making, and, ultimately, your financial reality. So, how do you rewrite your money script?

Reframing Your Perspective

Firstly, remember that your current financial situation is not your financial destiny. You're not 'broke' but experiencing a 'temporary lack of funds.' The latter phrase presents your situation as a passing challenge, an obstacle to overcome. It opens your mind to possibilities of change and growth rather than cementing it in a state of hopelessness.

Nurture an Abundance Mindset

The language of abundance doesn't focus on what's missing; it highlights what's present and anticipates what's coming. Rather than saying, "I can't afford that," try stating, "I choose to spend my money differently." This statement reiterates your control over your finances and promotes responsible decision-making. You're no longer a victim of your circumstances but a steward of your resources.

Speak in Affirmative Terms

Your subconscious mind is a powerful tool, but it cannot comprehend negatives. When you say, "I don't want to be in debt," your mind hears, "debt, debt, debt." Your subconscious mind *focuses on the subject matter*, for example, "DON'T think of a pink elephant." Did you think of a *pink elephant*? Remember, the subconscious mind doesn't know between what's good or bad. It just focuses on the subject and responds to your strongest emotions towards it. To effectively communicate with your subconscious, speak in affirmative terms, such as, "I am financially free" or "I am on my path to wealth creation."

Visualize and Verbalize Your Financial Goals

You've got to visualize your financial dreams with vivid details and speak them into existence. What's your grand money fantasy? Owning a swanky apartment in the city? Jet-setting around the world? Whatever it is, talk about it like it's already happening. Speak it into existence, like "I'm the boss of my own life" or "I'm sipping champagne in my penthouse suite." Feel it with details of your visions and embody the feelings as if you're acting the main role in a movie. When you paint a vivid picture, your subconscious works with your reticular activating system to make it a reality.

The power of visualization in actualizing goals is well-recognized, but equally important is the act of verbalization. Speak your financial goals into existence. When you articulate your ambitions, it crystallizes your intentions and sets the wheel of manifestation into motion.

Practice verbalizing positive financial outcomes. Say, "I am capable of earning a million dollars," or "I am on the path to financial freedom." By aligning your words with your desires, you're essentially programming your mind and reality toward achieving them.

Words in Action

Speaking the language of abundance harnesses the power of your words to reshape your attitudes, decisions, and behaviors concerning money. Your actions will naturally follow the direction of your words. Pair your positive dialogue with concrete actions. Build a savings plan, invest wisely, and enhance your financial education. As you align your words with actions, you'll notice a remarkable shift in your financial landscape.

In essence, the power to manifest abundance and wealth lies within you - in your thoughts, your words, and ultimately, your actions. When you realize that you are the master of your financial destiny, money ceases to be a stressor and becomes a tool - a means to realize your dreams, contribute to your community, and enhance your life's quality. So, be mindful of your language, nurture an abundance mindset, and let the symphony of your words orchestrate a future of financial prosperity. Embrace the power of your words as they command how money responds to you, shaping your reality one word at a time.

Next, let's move to mindset. The Law of Attraction stipulates that like energy attracts like energy. By cultivating a positive, prosperous mindset, you channel your life force energy towards attracting similar vibrations in the universe, drawing in abundance. Replace scarcity thinking with an abundance mindset. Affirmations are potent tools for this; statements like "I am prosperous" or "Money flows freely and abundantly to me" help attune your energy to the radio station of abundance.

There is an extraordinary power nestled within the simplicity of two words: "I AM." These two monosyllables, simple at first thought, form the bedrock of our reality and cast whatever to manifest with the colors of our self-perceptions. The truth is, the "I AM" within us wields a potent transformative power, a power often overlooked but can manifest your reality.

The phrase "I AM" is a complete sentence in itself, the shortest affirmation we can utter, yet it encapsulates our entire existence. It is a statement of identity, of existence, of being, and importantly, it is a pronouncement of conviction and affirmation about the self. These two words are the engine room, the power source from which we can draw to ignite and propel the vessel of our life's journey.

Every time we say "I AM," we are defining our reality—carving our individuality, underlining our strengths, and sometimes, unfortunately, reinforcing our perceived limitations. We are manifesting the narrative of our lives, either constructively or destructively. "I AM strong," "I AM successful," and "I AM happy" are as profoundly potent as "I AM weak," "I AM a failure," and "I AM unhappy."

The immense power of "I AM" lies in its infinite potentiality. It becomes a vessel that can carry whatever we decide to place within it. It is like a magical magnifier that amplifies the spell cast. Our unconscious mind does not distinguish between reality and imagination—it believes and acts upon whatever we affirm with our "I AM" statements.

Thus, our self-affirmations can shape our lives, our perceptions, and our reality. "I AM" can be a tool of immense self-empowerment, a weapon to combat negative self-perception and low self-esteem. It can help us rewrite our stories, heal old wounds, and lead us to the path of healing and personal growth.

Every "I AM" is a seed sown into the field of our minds. As we continue to water and nurture this seed with repetition and emotional intensity, it grows, sprouting into a new belief that directs our actions and behaviors. "I AM," therefore, forms the roots of our self-perception, shaping our attitudes and our experiences.

By consciously choosing empowering "I AM" affirmations, we can transform our world, cultivating self-love, confidence, resilience, and happiness. By continually affirming "I AM capable," we find ourselves undertaking challenges with courage and verve. By repeating "I AM deserving," we open ourselves to the abundance that the Universe has to offer. By stating "I AM love," we foster compassion and kindness within ourselves, changing how we interact with others.

The words "I AM" are a mirror, reflecting our thoughts, feelings, and beliefs. Depending on our chosen narrative, these reflections can either limit us or liberate us. The power of "I AM" allows us to consciously direct this narrative, leading us on a path to manifest our scripted reality.

Embrace the power of "I AM" affirmations. Cultivate a garden of positive thinking within your mind. Remember, you are the artist, the sculptor of your reality, and every "I AM" is a brushstroke, a chisel strike. Use them wisely, use them intently, and above all, use them lovingly. Because you are the person you choose to affirm through your "I AM" affirmations.

Recite your affirmations out loud every morning in the mirror, write them 10 times in the morning and evening, or repeat them in your mind throughout your days.

I AM AFFIRMATIONS:

1. "I AM a magnet for prosperity and wealth."
2. "I AM abundantly blessed and receive freely from the universe."
3. "I AM open to the limitless opportunities for financial success that surround me."
4. "I AM worthy of an abundant life, filled with richness and joy."
5. "I AM a channel through which prosperity flows."
6. "I AM attracting abundant health, wealth, and happiness into my life."
7. "I AM deserving of all the abundance that the universe has to offer."
8. "I AM financially free, living a life of abundance and prosperity."
9. "I AM a wealth creator, constantly drawing abundance towards me."
10. "I AM grateful for the unending abundance that fills my life."

You Are the Temple

Nurture your life force energy physically, too. Your body is the vessel that carries this energy, and its health directly influences your energy levels. Proper diet, regular exercise, and ample rest – are all crucial for maintaining a high energy level. Remember, a healthy body leads to a vibrant life force, which in turn attracts abundance.

Connecting with nature can also be a powerful way to enhance your life force energy. Spend time outdoors, feel the sun on your skin, breathe in the fresh air, and walk barefoot on the grass. These activities are grounding, helping you stay present and connected to the world around you, thereby recharging your life force energy. It's like plugging your life force directly into a power socket. Feel the sunshine, breathe in the freshness of crisp air, and walk barefoot on the soiled earth. It'll keep you grounded, fully charged, and ready to take on life with full force!

One of the most underrated yet incredibly potent tools at your disposal is quite literally beneath your feet. Grounding, also known as earthing, is the practice of reconnecting with the earth's natural energy, typically through direct contact with the ground.

To appreciate the connection between grounding and energy, we need to first acknowledge that money, in its purest form, is a flow of energy. The exchange of goods and services, the creation of wealth, and the accumulation of resources—all are transfers of energy. When you're in harmony with this universal flow, abundance comes naturally. Disconnection or disharmony, on the other hand, can block this flow from the Universe.

Grounding is all about re-establishing harmony and balance. It recalibrates our energy by connecting us to the earth's electromagnetic field—a limitless source of restorative power. By grounding ourselves, we align with the universal energy flow, where we can tune into positive energy and raise our life force energy.

Manifestation is a spiritual journey that starts from within. Many people visualize, set intentions, practice gratitude, and use affirmations—all powerful tools. However, without a clear, grounded energetic connection, these practices can sometimes fall short. Here's where grounding can catalyze and turbocharge your manifestation journey. The key to your manifestations is the frequency of your energy—on the spectrum between positive/high and negative/low.

When you ground yourself, you effectively clear away the energetic clutter. This practice releases 'static' from your energy field and cleanses it with a nature's shower. With this clarity and calmness, your intentions and visualizations can flow clearly. This open channel to the universe is a key part of manifesting your desired abundant energy.

The beauty of grounding is its simplicity. Here are some straightforward yet profound ways to practice it:

- **Barefoot Connection:** Walk barefoot on natural surfaces such as grass, sand, or soil. Feel the earth's energy seep into you, clearing away stress, anxiety, and negative energy.
- **Grounding Meditation:** Visualize roots extending from your feet into the earth, anchoring you securely. Feel the earth's energy rising, enveloping and filling you with stability and abundance.
- **Nature Immersion:** Spend time in natural environments. Embrace the forest's serenity, the ocean's expanse, or the mountain's majesty. Let the elemental energy cleanse and rejuvenate your spirit.
- **Grounding Foods:** Eat more root vegetables and foods rich in minerals, which promote a more grounded state.

While practicing these, mentally affirm your wealth intentions. Picture the money you desire to manifest as a stream of energy flowing towards you, drawn by your grounded state. Grounding's capacity to clear, stabilize, and align your energy puts you in harmony with the abundant flow of the universe. It's time we recognize grounding as a powerful catalyst for recharging our life force energy to manifest abundance. So, kick off those shoes, sink your toes into the soil, and get ready to ground your way to abundance.

Practicing gratitude is another potent method of raising your life force energy. When you express gratitude for what you have, you create a positive energy cycle that attracts more to be grateful for, including abundance. An attitude of gratitude sends a signal to the universe that you're ready for more blessings.

Finally, direct your enhanced life force energy toward your specific goals. Visualization can be an effective tool for this. Imagine the wealth and abundance you wish to attract. See it in vivid detail, feel it in your hands, and live the experience in your mind. This exercise supercharges your life force energy with the power of vivid visualization, making it a magnet for attracting what you desire.

The human mind is an incredible work of evolutionary artistry. Its labyrinthine neural networks shape our realities, in concert with our life experiences, perceptions, beliefs, and emotions. However, we often fail to acknowledge an astounding feature of this mental kaleidoscope— the unconscious mind's inability to distinguish between reality and imagination.

First, let's journey through the neural alleyways of our minds to understand this fascinating phenomenon. When we experience an event, a series of neurons fire together, creating a pathway. The more we relive the event, the stronger the pathway becomes—akin to a well-trodden trail in the forest. Now, when we vividly imagine a scenario, the mind evokes similar neural pathways as if the event were happening in our current reality. Thus, the line between the tangible and intangible blurs for the unconscious mind.

This conflation between reality and imagination opens a world of possibilities for us. This is where visualization comes in to manifest your wildest dreams into a reality. Visualization, put simply, is the act of creating compelling and vivid pictures in your mind. It is the conscious use of this inherent trait of our unconscious mind to manifest our desired outcomes— in this context, abundance.

Consider the workings of a champion athlete. Before the performance, they spend considerable time mentally rehearsing every jump, every swing, and every maneuver. They embody the win in their mind before it unfolds in reality. This visualization practice bridges the gap between their current state and their desired outcome.

To apply this concept to our quest for abundance, we must understand that wealth extends beyond the monetary realm—it encompasses a richness of experience, knowledge, relationships, health, and, indeed, money.

Start by creating a 'rich' vision. What does abundance look like to you? A satisfying job, a comfortable home, fulfilling relationships, robust health, and travels around the world? Paint a mental image as vivid as possible and use your senses—smell the air, feel the emotions, hear the sounds, etc. Once you have this image, bring it to your mind's forefront repeatedly. Every morning when you wake up and every night before you sleep, find a quiet space, close your eyes, and live in this dream reality you've imagined. Feel the joy, satisfaction, and abundance, and embody it.

But how do we go from visualization to a quantum leap into wealth? At its core, quantum physics tells us that our universe is composed of energy and probabilities. Every potential reality exists simultaneously as a 'quantum state' until observed or measured. By visualizing and embodying abundance, you are choosing this reality from the field of infinite possibilities. You collapse the quantum wave function into a particle of wealth reality.

Does it mean wealth will suddenly fall from the sky? No. Instead, your actions, decisions, and perceptions will begin to align with this new reality you've envisioned. You'll find opportunities that were always there but unseen due to your prior mindset. The universe around you responds and adjusts. This is where you'll suddenly run into more coincidences, synchronicities, and serendipities, which are signs from the universe that guide you on the right path.

Visualization is a manifestation tool that reshapes your mindset and rewires your brain to create an environment conducive to embodying abundance that feels like your new normal state of being—meaning feeling more and more comfortable with abundance so that when it arrives, you can receive it with ease. It's the difference between the feelings of "wanting and chasing" and shifting to feelings of "being abundant NOW." The quantum leap is a series of aligned actions, brought together by the magnet of your vivid visualization, pulling you inexorably towards your envisioned abundant dreams.

Remember, the unconscious mind acts upon what it believes. Give it a compelling belief to act upon. Use visualization as your movie to create your life of abundance and experience the thrill of quantum leaping to wealth. Your reality is waiting to be transformed.

Visualization is like daydreaming but with a purpose. Imagine what it feels like to have all the wealth you desire. Feel the plush rug under your bare feet in your dream home, the adrenaline rush as you seal that killer deal, and the warmth of loved ones laughing around a dinner table. Make it real. See it, feel it, smell it, and most importantly, BE in it NOW, embody it fully with every cell in your body. You're planting these images into your mind. Like a skilled gardener, you're seeding your future success. You're setting up the blueprint for your future to follow. You'll notice a shift in your actions, choices, and attitudes that align you with the world of abundance you've been visualizing. You'll start spotting opportunities you never saw before because now, you're wearing your glasses from the future version of you. That also means making decisions from a place of your future self. Visualization is a mental workout that primes your brain to act like you're already living in abundance. The quantum leap is being your future self in the present moment by thinking, feeling, embodying, and being the future version of yourself in the *NOW*. It's a path paved with actions, thoughts, and decisions, all bathed in the light of your vivid visualizations.

Enhance your visualizations with mind movies. Mind movies are a manifestation tool to rocket fuel your visualizations and dream life. A mind movie is like a vision board in a short video form. It's a dynamic, cinematic experience that engages your mind, fuels your emotions, and propels your manifestations into the stratosphere. By creating a mind movie, you're not just visualizing your dream life—you're living it in your mind, feeling it in your soul, and setting the stage for it to unfold in your reality.

Step 1: Script Your Dream Life

Every great movie starts with a killer script, and your mind movie is no exception. This is your chance to get crystal clear about what you want to manifest. Grab a pen and paper, or fire up your laptop and start writing the screenplay of your dream life.

Get specific. Where are you living? What does your home look like? Who are you with? What does your day-to-day routine involve? What kind of work are you doing? How do you feel? Paint a vivid picture with your words, and don't hold back. This is your masterpiece.

Step 2: Gather Your Visuals

Now that you've written the script, it's time to bring it to life with images. Think of this as casting the perfect scenes for your movie. Scour the internet, magazines, or your own photo library for images that represent your dreams. Find pictures of your dream house, your ideal job, the places you want to travel, and the lifestyle you aspire to live.

Pro tip: Choose images that evoke strong emotions. The more these images resonate with your desires, the more powerful your mind movie will be. You want to feel the excitement, joy, and fulfillment these images represent.

Step 3: Choose Your Soundtrack

Every epic movie needs a beautiful soundtrack. Choose music that inspires you, uplifts you, and matches your dream life. This soundtrack should make your heart race with excitement and your spirit soar.

Whether it's a motivational anthem, a serene instrumental, or a high-energy pop song, the right music will amplify the emotional impact of your mind movie and help embed those feelings deep into your subconscious.

Step 4: Bring It All Together

It's time to put the pieces together and create your cinematic master-piece. There are various tools and apps available for creating videos—choose one that's user-friendly and suits your needs. Upload your images, add your soundtrack, and arrange everything in a way that tells the story of your dream life. Also, include text with affirmations such as "I am rich" and "I am successful," etc. Infuse it with positive affirmations and empowering statements. These can be text overlays on your images or voiceovers that narrate your journey. The goal is to make this experience as immersive and inspiring as possible.

Step 5: Watch and Feel

Your mind movie is ready for its debut! Find a quiet, comfortable space, and play your mind movie. As you watch, fully immerse yourself in the experience. Feel the emotions as if everything you're seeing is already your reality. Bask in the joy, excitement, and gratitude of living your dream life. Be in its energy now and embody the feelings in every cell of your body!

Make it a daily ritual to watch your mind movie, especially in the morning and before bed. These times are when your subconscious mind is most receptive. The more you watch, the more you'll program your mind to align with your desires, making your manifestations inevitable.

Step 6: Take Inspired Action

A mind movie is a powerful tool, but you still need to take action. Let your mind movie serve as a compass, guiding you towards inspired actions that bring you closer to your dreams. Pay attention to the opportunities and ideas that come your way, and act on them with confidence and determination.

Your mind movie is in your back pocket any time you need inspiration or a reminder of your dream goals. It will keep you focused, motivated, and aligned with your highest vision, but it's up to you to make it happen in the real world. Show up, do the work, and watch as your dreams unfold.

Live Your Blockbuster Life

Creating a mind movie is like giving your dreams a backstage pass to your subconscious mind and asking the DJ to program your future reality with your mind movie soundtrack. It's a vibrant, emotional, and energetically powerful way to keep your vision alive and thriving. By watching your mind movie regularly, you're rewiring your brain, raising your vibration, and magnetizing the life you desire.

So, go ahead and create your mind movie masterpiece. Watch it, feel it, and let it propel you towards your most magnificent reality. You have the power to manifest anything you desire, and your blockbuster dream life is waiting for its star—you to rise as your highest authentic self.

Your mind is the ultimate believer. It will act on the reality it believes in. So give it a belief that makes you feel like a shining star. Let your imagination be the key to unlocking your reality of abundance. So dream your wildest dreams and visualize them so intensely that you cry tears of joy!

Your life force energy is not just the essence of your existence; it's the energy that flows and shapes your reality. By nurturing and channeling it properly, you can attract immense abundance into your life. Remember, abundance is something you tune into, and that flows from the Universe. By raising your life force energy, you align yourself with the frequency of positive energy to attract abundance. It's your river, your energy, your life force; make it flow toward the ocean of abundance.

28

Energy Cleansing

Every morning, when the sun rises, it gives you an opportunity to rise anew like the sun. A chance to tap into the profound light within you and make a change on any new given day the sun rises. This energy has the power to attract positivity, happiness, and, ultimately, abundance. Harnessing and enhancing it calls for a process of internal cleansing, a journey toward holistic well-being.

The first step in this journey is understanding the concept of energy frequency. Much like the electromagnetic waves radiating from your radio, every individual emits a specific vibrational frequency. This frequency, shaped by your thoughts, emotions, and physical well-being, attracts experiences and people of similar energy into your life. As per the Law of Attraction, like attracts like. Therefore, when you tune your energy to higher frequencies of joy, gratitude, and love, you attract similar energies that can come in the form of a grateful friend, a free coffee, or finding a dime on the floor!

This invisible energy is not only around us but within us, pulsing through every cell, every thought, and every emotion. We are, at our essence, beings of energy. And just like a river can be polluted or remain crystal clear, our personal energy can also experience similar senses. As we journey through life, we may find ourselves ensnared in situations or with individuals that deplete our energy, leaving us feeling heavy, drained, or disconnected from our true essence. It is here that the art of energetic cleansing plays a crucial role.

Energetic cleansing is the practice of purifying your personal energy, restoring vitality, and realigning with the highest expression of your true self. Much like the act of washing your physical body, energetic cleansing allows you to wash away emotional debris and spiritual pollutants, providing a fresh slate upon which you can manifest and create.

Energetic cleansing is a deeply personal and introspective journey. It is as much about discarding what no longer serves you as it is about understanding why those energies were attracted to you in the first place. Your energy is your responsibility. In cleansing it, you're taking care of your energy and enabling you to shape it with consciousness and intentionality.

There is a myriad of ways to cleanse your energy that resonates differently with different individuals. Here are some effective practices you may wish to integrate into your life:

Mindful Meditation: Find a quiet, comfortable space where you can be alone with your thoughts. As you relax and breathe deeply, visualize a gentle, radiant light washing over you, clearing away any stagnant or negative energy.

Nature Immersion: Nature is a powerful purifier. Spend time in nature or by bodies of water. Imagine the wind carrying away your worries and the water washing away any energy blockages.

Sound Healing: Sound frequencies can be used to recalibrate our energy fields. Experiment with singing bowls, chimes, drums, or healing music.

Physical Movement: Practices like yoga, tai chi, or even dance can help shake off stale energy and promote a healthy energy flow throughout your body.

Energy Healing Practices: Reiki, acupuncture, and other energy healing modalities can help remove energy blockages and promote balance and well-being.

Affirmations and Positive Self-Talk: Affirmations are a powerful way to reclaim your energetic sovereignty. Create a set of positive statements that resonate with you and repeat them daily. Repeating positive affirmations can help to reprogram your subconscious mind and shift your energy. Choose or create affirmations that resonate with you, and make it a habit to repeat them daily.

Energy Cleansing Methods:

1. Visualization: One of the most simple and effective methods of cleansing energy is through visualization. Sit comfortably, close your eyes, and imagine a bright light emanating from within your body, radiating outwards and purifying your energy field. This light could be any color you feel drawn to, although white light is often associated with purification and healing.

2. Breathwork: Conscious breathing is a powerful tool for energy cleansing. Practices such as yoga or breathwork effectively use the breath to move and clear energy in the body.

3. Smudging: This ancient practice involves burning sacred herbs such as sage, cedar, or palo santo and using the smoke to cleanse one's energy. Please ensure that you follow proper safety protocols and are aware of sustainability concerns.

4. Epsom Salt Baths: Epsom salts have been used for centuries to cleanse and recharge the body's energy. Soak in a warm bath with a cup or two of Epsom salts for about 20 minutes to help cleanse your aura and rejuvenate your energy.

5. Energy Healing Techniques: Modalities such as Reiki can cleanse your energy field. These methods often require a certified practitioner, although you can learn to perform some of these techniques yourself with proper training.

6. Chakra Balancing: This method focuses on the seven primary energy centers in your body or chakras. There are various ways to cleanse and balance your chakras, including meditation, sound therapy, yoga, and the use of crystals.

7. Grounding: Grounding techniques, such as walking barefoot in nature, can help to discharge negative energy and rebalance your energetic field. The simple act of physically touching the earth can be a powerful energy cleanser.

8. Sound Therapy: Certain sound frequencies are believed to resonate with our energy fields and can help to cleanse and harmonize our energy. This could involve listening to specific music, using a singing bowl, or chanting specific mantras.

9. Crystals: Different types of crystals have different properties that can help to cleanse, balance, and recharge your energy. Some popular options include clear quartz for general energy cleansing, black tourmaline for protection from negative energy, and amethyst for spiritual growth and healing.

Different methods will resonate with different people. Trust your intuition as you explore these techniques and find the ones that work best for you. Remember that consistency is key—energetic hygiene is most effective when it becomes a regular part of your routine.

- Mindfulness is a potent tool for tuning into your present moment and observing the nature of your thoughts. This observation allows you to recognize patterns that do not serve your highest good. Meditation, an extension of mindfulness, helps you break free from these patterns by creating a space for tranquility and connection with your higher self.
- Physical well-being is intrinsically tied to energy levels. Exercise, a balanced diet, and adequate sleep provide the body with the necessary fuel to maintain high energy frequencies. Practices such as yoga and Tai Chi, which bridge the physical and spiritual, can be particularly effective.
- Methods such as Reiki, acupuncture, and sound therapy target energy blockages and facilitate the free flow of life force within you. With regular practice, these techniques have the potential to significantly uplift your energy frequencies.

To raise your frequency, it's essential to focus on positivity and feeling grateful for the blessings in your life. Gratitude changes your brain's chemistry, releasing dopamine and serotonin, the feel-good neurotransmitters. This shift results in a higher vibrational frequency that resonates with abundance.

The brain does not clearly distinguish between imagined and real events, a fact that you can use to your advantage. Spend a few moments each day visualizing yourself as wealthy. See it, feel it, believe it, and embody it. Your brain will begin to work towards this reality, and your energy will align with this vision.

In this practice of cleansing and renewal, you become an active participant in the universal flow, shaping and shifting your reality with the power of intention. As your energy becomes clearer, your ability to manifest your desires becomes stronger. You step into alignment with the highest version of yourself, glowing with the light of your authentic power. Remember, energetic cleansing is not a one-time task but an ongoing process, a spiritual hygiene practice, if you will. Life is dynamic and ever-changing, and so are the energies we interact with. By maintaining a regular practice of energy cleansing, you are not only liberating yourself from past burdens but are also paving the way for new, positive energies to enter your life.

The journey to cleanse your energy is not a one-time event but a continual process. You're not just brushing your teeth once in your lifetime; you're brushing them every morning and evening. The same goes for your energy; check the gunk that got picked up throughout the day and protect your energy by fueling up with positive energy every morning with exercise, meditation, yoga, etc. Nurture the positive, weed out the negative, and allow your vibration to vibrate high. As you raise your frequency and bask in happiness, holistic abundance will permeate every aspect of your life.

As you clear your energy field, you'll find more space, clarity, and alignment with your higher self. This alignment is the magic key that unlocks the door to abundance. You'll find your actions more purposeful, your decision-making more aligned, and your path toward your goals clearer. Remember, energy is infectious; the energy you radiate will attract the same kind of energy back to you. If you vibrate at the frequency of positivity and abundance, that's what the Universe will echo back. Keep in mind that energy does not lie! Be guided by your light, protect your energy field, and create a ritual around cleansing and recalibrating your energy. When you become the master of your energy, you become the master of your life, capable of manifesting a life beyond your wildest dreams.

29

Self-Love

The secret to our money relationship which lies in valuing our self-worth. Low self-worth can be a sneaky saboteur of financial success, whispering insidious tales of unworthiness when it comes to wealth and abundance. Unfortunately, some of us are unwittingly carrying around beliefs that are like anchors, dragging down our ability to manifest financial prosperity. Learning to value ourselves and our unique skills and talents is essential in cultivating a sense of deservingness to receive abundance. When we believe in our worth and capabilities, we naturally attract opportunities for more abundance. The magic lies in reprogramming that mighty subconscious mind. In this transformational alchemy, we rise above those constraints, unleashing our full potential to tap into the boundless abundance that's just waiting to transform our lives.

It is essential to understand that your net worth does not define your true value. You are inherently worthy, just as you are, and cultivating self-love is the key to unlocking the doors to abundance in all aspects of your life. Self-love, at its core, is the unshakable belief that you are deserving of all the goodness life has to offer. It is not about arrogance or self-centeredness; rather, it is a compassionate acceptance of your whole self—the good, the bad, and the imperfect. Embracing self-love means celebrating your unique soul and acknowledging your blunders with kindness, for they are an inherent part of being human.

The relationship we have with money is intimately tied to our self-perception. If we feel unworthy, guilty, or shameful about our financial situation, we inadvertently create barriers to prosperity. Negative self-talk can become a self-fulfilling prophecy, leading us to make poor financial choices or hesitate to pursue lucrative opportunities.

On the contrary, those who embrace self-love approach financial matters from a place of empowerment. They understand that their worthiness is not tied to their bank account balance. Instead, they value themselves regardless of their financial status. This mindset allows them to set clear financial goals, pursue careers that align with their passions, and invest in their dreams with unwavering faith.

When you nurture self-love, you detach your self-worth from external markers of success. You no longer seek validation externally from material possessions or societal norms. This newfound freedom empowers you to believe in yourself, seize opportunities, and embrace growth without the fear of failure. You become a magnet for abundance, attracting prosperity and wealth into your life.

Furthermore, self-love helps you recognize that abundance is your birthright. There is more than enough to go around for everyone, and you have the power to create the financial reality you desire. Instead of viewing money as a scarce resource that only a select few can attain, see it as an infinite and abundant flow from the Universe. It is about nurturing the foundation of love within yourself. As you cultivate self-love, you will find that your financial health improves, but more importantly, your life will flourish, and your overall well-being will soar to new heights.

In the depths of our being lies an invaluable treasure: our mental mind. Like a crown adorned with precious gems, it has the power to elevate us to our highest potential, empower us, and enrich every aspect of our lives. Practice mental sovereignty and reclaim your power to manifest abundance by choosing peace in every circumstance. It's a declaration that you deserve the best life has to offer, and that begins with nurturing your innermost self.

Just as a king or queen governs their kingdom wisely, so must we exercise authority over your inner realm. The outside world may often seem chaotic, but by establishing inner harmony, you can better navigate life's storms that come your way. Choose serenity as a guiding force for a life of true abundance.

Every quest carries its challenges, and the path to mental sovereignty is no different. Negative thoughts may try to undermine your confidence, fear may cast its shadow on your decisions, and past wounds may hold you captive in their memories. Yet, be not disheartened, for each challenge is an opportunity for transcendence. Transmute every challenge to be a treasure of wisdom. With every hurdle you overcome, you grow stronger, your crown shines brighter, and your power to manifest abundance magnifies. Embrace the challenges, for they are the chisels that sculpt your inner self into a masterpiece of inner power and wisdom.

To claim your crown, you must unravel the illusions that cloud your perception. Often, we let external circumstances dictate our emotions, losing sight of the fact that true power lies within. By recognizing that our thoughts are malleable, we liberate ourselves from the shackles of negativity. At the heart of your crown is the most valuable gem— peace. In the stillness of peace, your mind becomes a fertile ground for abundant manifestations. Like a tranquil lake reflecting the moon's glow, a peaceful mind will radiate to your external reality by reflecting your peaceful energy. Choosing peace is an act of self-love. It is recognizing that you have the power to steer your thoughts away from turmoil and toward serenity. The outside world may be chaotic, but your inner world remains a sanctuary you can always return to as a haven of tranquility.

In the presence of peace, the vibrations of positivity resonate, and the law of attraction reflects your tune. Abundance becomes a natural consequence of aligning your thoughts with the Universe's boundless potential. Manifesting abundance encompasses all aspects of life—love, joy, fulfillment, and purpose. When your crown shines with the brilliance of mental sovereignty, you attract abundance effortlessly. By embracing your worthiness, you open the floodgates of prosperity. Trust that you are deserving of the abundance that flows towards you and that the universe conspires to fulfill your heart's desires.

In the end, remember that your mental health is the birth of all your thoughts. Your thoughts are the seeds in your garden of life. Plant positive seeds in your mind to have a flourishing healthy mind and bring about a flourishing healthy life. By choosing peace behind every intention, you will gain inner peace to feel good with abundance. With your crown of mental sovereignty, you possess the key to unlock the treasures of life. Transcend from challenges, appreciate the journey, and choose peace as you manifest the abundant life of your dreams.

30

One with the Universe

A sky full of stars, a notion so vast and infinite that it stretches beyond our comprehension. Each twinkling point of light is a symbol of the Universe's majestic, limitless abundance.

The Universe is a mysterious, boundless, invisible energy. It's not static; it's dynamic, ever-expanding, continuously forming new galaxies, stars, and planets. This constant creation, this infinite expanse, echoes the principle of abundance. The Universe, in its very essence, is a creative force, constantly birthing new forms, experiences, and possibilities.

When we understand this facet of the Universe, we awaken to the truth that it's not about clutching tightly or hoarding out of scarcity but rather about generously giving, actively creating, and joyfully expanding our energy. When we resonate with this frequency of expansion, we start to mirror it in our lives, resulting in abundance. The state of lack, of not having enough, is a mere illusion, a blinkered perception that disconnects us from the cosmic truth of limitless abundance.

Now, one might ask, how can we tap into this abundant Universe? The secret lies in recognizing that you, yourself, are an integral part of this abundant Universe. Like a wave in the ocean, you are not separate from the Universe. You are an expression of the Universe, a manifestation of its creation through the creativity of the Source, and therefore, you share in its infinite abundance that originates from the Source.

To attune yourself to this Source of universal abundance, you must first shift your mindset. Let go of the fears of scarcity and the anxieties of not having enough and replace them with the realization of limitless potential and creativity of the Universe. Embrace a perspective of abundance, an understanding that there is always more than enough for all. This shift is not merely intellectual; it should permeate your thoughts, feelings, actions, and energy. When you view the world through the lens of abundance, it will shift your energy and invite abundance into your life.

The practice of gratitude is a powerful magnet for abundance. When you express appreciation for what you already have, you align your energy with the abundant frequencies of the Universe, effortlessly attracting even greater abundance into your reality. By being thankful, you align yourself with the frequency of abundance, and the Universe responds in kind, presenting you with more reasons to be grateful.

Finally, give freely. As you give, you receive. The act of giving, whether it is love, time, knowledge, or resources, creates an abundant flow of energy to ignite a powerful current of abundance to surge through the vast field of potential. This flow attracts more abundance to you like the law of cause and effect. The more you give authentically, the more you receive in an ever-expanding cycle of abundance.

Abundance is the Source of the Universe and the cosmic truth. Once we understand and align with this truth, we become the master creators of our lives. By aligning our energy to the tune of the Source of the abundant Universe, we open the floodgates to the Universe's infinite possibilities to manifest in our lives, creating a reality that is as expansive and magnificent as the Universe itself.

31

Notes

References:

Mani, Anandi, Sendhil Mullainathan, Eldar Shafir, and Jiaying Zhao. "Poverty Impedes Cognitive Function." Science 341, no. 6149 (2013): 976-980. https://doi.org/10.1126/science.1238041.

Damasio, Antonio R. *Descartes' Error: Emotion, Reason, and the Human Brain.* G.P. Putnam's Sons, 1994.

32

Resources

Learn:
https://www.khanacademy.org/college-careers-more/financial-literacy

About the Author

❤✕ 🅣🅗🅐🅝🅚 🅨🅞🅤 ❤✕

You can connect with me on:
🌐 https://linktr.ee/aesthetixgiftshop